DATE DUE			

ACADEMIC SOCIALISM

ALSO BY MICHAEL J. BUGEJA

POETRY

WHAT WE DO FOR MUSIC
THE VISIONARY
PLATONIC LOVE *(AN ORCHISES BOOK)*
FLIGHT FROM VALHALLA
AFTER OZ *(AN ORCHISES BOOK)*

ESSAYS

CULTURE'S SLEEPING BEAUTY
THE ART AND CRAFT OF POETRY
POET'S GUIDE

ACADEMIC SOCIALISM

MERIT AND MORALE IN HIGHER EDUCATION

MICHAEL J. BUGEJA

ORCHISES • WASHINGTON • 1994

Copyright © 1994 by Michael J. Bugeja

Library of Congress Cataloging in Publication Data

Bugeja, Michael J.
    Academic socialism : merit and morale in higher education / Michael
J. Bugeja
        p. cm.
    Includes bibliographical references and index.
    ISBN 0-914061-42-9 : $22.95
        1. Education, Higher —United States—Administration 2. Education-
al accountability—United States 3. Education, Higher—United States—
Aims and objectives. 4. College teachers—United States—Attitudes.
5. Educational surveys—United States.
        I. Title.
    LB2341.B74   1994
        378.1'00973—dc20   94-3932
                                                    CIP

Manufactured in the United States of America

Published by Orchises Press
P. O. Box 20602
Alexandria
Virginia
22320-1602

G6E4C2A

The times have no heart. The true reform can be undertaken any
morning before unbarring our doors.

—HENRY DAVID THOREAU

To

DIANE

CONTENTS

II
Rainbow of Responses

ACKNOWLEDGEMENTS

Much of the immediate thinking for this book comes from my teaching and writing in the Journalism programs at Ohio University and, to a lesser extent, Oklahoma State University. As all essayists must, I have drawn from my own and others' experiences as reported to me for anecdotes and examples that I believe have a significance beyond these two noble institutions. Although I hope that the second half of this book, to which people from numerous institutions generously contributed, will substantiate my more general claims, I would be remiss if I didn't acknowledge the support of Ohio University for providing me with a rich, diverse, and sometimes trying experience in academe.

Ohio University also is to be praised for giving me time to write this study. No business, even the gutsy media that embraces the First Amendment, would encourage an author to investigate problems and suggest solutions. This is testament to the value of academic freedom, a concept in which administrators and professors—some of whom would dispute my ideas—believe deeply.

On a personal level, I give special thanks to my research assistant and wife Diane Sears-Bugeja who spent weeks organizing and evaluating boxes of surveys and running computer analyses. I want to thank these colleagues and friends: Paul Nelson, Ralph Izard, E.E. Chang, Diane Campbell, Josep Rota, Judith Lee, Sue Dewine, Marilyn Greenwald, Guido Stempel, Alden Waitt, Heido Sacko, and Cassandra Reese who provided information and encouragement.

I also should acknowledge dozens of others at Ohio University and other campuses who provided information and off-the-record interviews. In addition, these business leaders and educators returned surveys with minor or no comments but gave permission to use their names as study-participants: Jim Barnes, Northeast Missouri State University; James Bogan, University of Missouri-Rolla; Bob Cairns, district manager, Columbia Gas of Ohio; Tom Chandler, Rhode Island School of Design; Kelly Cherry, University of Wisconsin-Madison; Emanuel Di Pasquale, Middlesex County College, New Jersey; Stephen Dixon, Johns Hopkins, writing seminars; James Haddon, Managing Director,

Paine-Webber Group, New York City; David Hopes, University of North Carolina at Asheville; Fleda Brown Jackson, University of Delaware; David Lee, Southern Utah University; Laurence Lieberman, University of Illinois; Ed Ochester, University of Pittsburgh; Richard Peabody, continuing education programs at universities of Virginia and Maryland and at Georgetown; Stuart Peterfreund, Northeastern University, Boston; Robert Pinsky, Boston University; Peter Platten, President and CEO, Valley Bancorporation, Appleton, Wisconsin; Mike Pletcher, manager, Atco Sheltered Workshop, Athens County; James Ruppert, University of Alaska-Fairbanks; Jim Simmerman, Northern Arizona University; Joseph Somoza, New Mexico State University; Ronald Wallace, University of Wisconsin-Madison; Larry Woiwode, SUNY-Binghamton.

Respondents who did not wish to be identified included several CEOs of Fortune 500 companies and a Pulitzer Prize and several Guggenheim-winning writers.

I also want to express my gratitude to the editors of *The Midwest Quarterly* who published my essay "Academic Socialism," upon which this book is based, and to Roger Lathbury, publisher of Orchises Press, whose encouragement continues to motivate me.

Finally, I thank my students who renew my intellectual life each quarter. It is with love and admiration for them that I meet the challenges of proposing education reform, convinced that they deserve better.

MICHAEL J. BUGEJA
ATHENS, OHIO

PART ONE

MAKING MY CASE

═══════════════════════════════════

One

ACADEMIC SOCIALISTS

Socialism has often given rise to a statist politics, committed to replacing mutual aid with bureaucratic benevolence. That indeed is the record of Communist regimes, except that the bureaucrats never turn out to be benevolent.

MICHAEL WALZER in *The New Republic*

WORK EXPERIENCE

I've been a professor for more than 15 years, almost twice as long as I was a working journalist. Once I had an exciting, exhausting career as a reporter and editor for United Press International. That company may be out of business by the time you read this, or it may not, because UPI seems to teeter each year on the brink of collapse.

UPI is a wire service. It owns or rents a string of bureaus

throughout the world. Reporters file news items around the clock. The typical reporter for a major newspaper like *The New York Times* might do a story or two per week; wire service reporters file several dozen. Our motto at UPI was: "Get it first, get it fast, get it right." We were a profit-making organization, although we seldom made a profit. Our chief competitor was the Associated Press, a non-profit company, which usually outspent and outstaffed us. For instance, I was a bureau manager in charge of two huge states, North and South Dakota, and was outstaffed by the AP 13 to 3. But we kept pace. We did so by working 60-hour weeks on average, violating union rules, receiving no overtime. Managers like me promised "comp time"—or an hour off for every one worked without pay over forty per week. No one got comp time, of course; oh, an hour or a day or two sporadically, perhaps, if there was a family emergency or illness that coincided with a lull in the news. We all knew that comp time was a joke.

Because the AP didn't have to make a profit, it could offer reporters easier hours and better raises than ours. Some years we did not have any raise at all. Simply, there was no money. We were continually on "downhold," which meant holding down costs. Toward the end of my UPI career, I could no longer afford to pay a journalism student minimum wage to take high school scores on Friday and Saturday nights. I had to come in to work then, after laboring my 60 hours. I also had to come in on weekday mornings at 4 a.m. to file cattle markets and weather advisories. At the end of the month, I would try to pay bills and meet my budget. On occasion I did so by paying half of my telephone bills, daring Ma Bell to sue UPI; she never did.

Our AP counterparts questioned why we worked so hard under such terrible conditions.

The answer was simple: *to beat you, dummy.*

We were the few, the proud, the "UniPressers." Our mascot was "The Stringer," an underpaid radio jock or weekly newspaper hack who wanted a byline with our logo and who would call in stories from around the state, receiving $1 per each *edited* inch of copy. After a stringer would file his or her story, we would thank them profusely and make them feel that they were as famous as Peter Jennings or as sharp as Ellen Goodman.

Good managers treated their reporters with similar respect. When an employee like Melanie Rigney, an editor now at *Ad Age,* would find the time to write and file a feature story on her one day off in ten, I would spend an extra hour at the bureau, polishing her piece and then pulling rank on the copy desk person in New York, convincing him or her to run it on the national wire so that Melanie would have a chance at appearing in the Sunday *Times.* At any rate, managers in cities like Boston or Chicago or Los Angeles would clip her story from local newspapers and send them to her in Sioux Falls with cheery notes of congratulations. Reporters across the country would send "kudos" on the message wire. Melanie's morale would increase and offset some of her stress.

In sum, UPI management knew that morale was the chief reason that the company was still in business. Our top executives then—H.L. Stevenson, editor-in-chief, and Don Reed, managing editor—were as busy as bureau managers and reporters, trying to keep us out of bankruptcy court. Yet they, too, took time to send us a personal thank-you letter or critique our copy on the message wire. (I cherish a thank-you letter from Stevenson complimenting me for disclosing that the swine flu shot in 1976 was causing paralysis—the top story of my career.)

Sure, UniPressers complained about their salaries. Sure, they whined or threatened to strike when faced with another year of token or no raises. And yes, some of us burned out or lost husbands or wives to divorce or got ill with the stress and the long hours. These are *moral,* not morale, problems.

But my UPI experience taught me important lessons about morale. I learned that employees want to be appreciated at least as much as they want to be paid. UniPressers actually believed that the free world would suffer if our company went out of business, allowing the AP to monopolize the news. We were protectors of the Republic, defenders of the faith.

We relied on teamwork to beat our opponent. Each night when Don Reed sent out the "logs"—a scorecard that tallied the daily saga between UPI and AP—our hearts beat a little faster with the tickertape: *Bugeja, swine flu, 19-0.* (This log meant that newspapers subscribing to both wires used my story in a shut-out of the AP.) Logs also bolstered morale. We measured ourselves by those numbers the way brokers do portfolios by the Dow. When our numbers went down, our resolve went up. We competed with the AP *and* ourselves.

One either married UPI or a person.

I quit the wire service in 1979 to marry Diane Sears, a part-time UPI photographer and full-time social worker. We both agreed that our erratic hours would doom a relationship. So we left Sioux Falls and headed south to Oklahoma State University.

RETURN TO ACADEME

I took a $5,500 pay cut and a job as adviser to the campus newspaper. Diane enrolled in the Graduate Program in the Journalism School, where I also taught part-time. I already had a master's in mass communications from South Dakota State, so I entered the doctoral program in English. By 1986 I had my Ph.D. in creative writing and was tenured and promoted in my home department.

The transition did not go smoothly, however. The state of Oklahoma was coming off the oil boom of the late 1970s and in the early 1980s crashed economically. As happened during my employment at UPI, there were token or no raises for several years. Professors were working long hours, teaching more classes or ones with higher enrollments. My director, Marlan Nelson, tried as hard as he could to keep up morale, but lacked support from the university administration and the Legislature. In fact, a few lawmakers justified cuts in higher education by accusing professors of being underworked and overpaid.

That message went over well with taxpayers. They couldn't afford higher taxes anyway, given their own frozen wages or worse— unemployment—so politicians in Oklahoma City bore down hard on academe. Soon professors themselves were accusing each other, wanting to be appreciated for their contributions, but doing so at their colleagues' expense. Some elevated research over teaching or publications over service or extension over student evaluations, vying for a symbolic 1 percent merit raise. Reputations were damaged, friendships lost, for a few hundred dollars.

I had had enough. Unable to tolerate another summer without employment, one morning in late May I strode to the "hanging file," an appropriate metaphor: a clip board on the wall announcing job opportunities at other universities. I tore off the first listing: a journalism professorship at Ohio University. I applied and got the post and relocated to Athens two months later.

By now I was desperate. For seven years I had struggled to feed my family between June 1 and October 1, months without pay. So I took the Ohio position with a $500 pay cut at the associate rank, but with the promise of regular summer employment. That meant a net $4,000 more per year. I was told that I couldn't receive a higher salary because my appointment might run into problems at Affirmative Action. (Two women also were being hired at the assistant professor rank for similarly low salaries.) Yet Ohio would not be like Oklahoma, I was assured. Professors here were receiving annual raises between 6 and 8 percent, so in the long run I would be better off in Athens than in Stillwater. Moreover, the E.W. Scripps School was one of the top journalism programs in the country (according, ironically, to the Associated Press).

For the most part, the rosy forecast held between 1986 and 1988. Raises were regular. Morale at the Scripps School was good. Faculty meetings went smoothly and everyone contributed as a team. OU reminded me of UPI. Everyone praised each other or at least made jokes about each other when we disapproved of a colleague's easy hours or impossible standards.

Then the economy caught up with Ohio. Raises sank to 3 and then 2 percent and finally to nothing. Our governor and Legislature began attacking academe, as lawmakers had done in Oklahoma, to justify budget cuts to the overtaxed and underemployed public.

Morale at the Journalism School sank as it had at Oklahoma. A few colleagues began bickering with each other, elevating research above teaching or advising above service, gossiping about each other and politicking in the halls. Some years annual reviews made little sense, with a few profs getting fair marks for publishing when they hadn't published at all and others getting poor marks for publishing when they had (but not on the right topics).

Our attitude changed from good to bad with the economy. Instead of lauding each other's contributions, celebrating the diversity of ideas that had won awards for our school, some of us turned on each other. This was happening across campus, across the state. We didn't need politicians to bash us because we were bashing ourselves. But our timing was convenient for legislators in Columbus who wanted to freeze taxes and our salaries and work us harder than before.

Our spirits sank as class enrollments rose.

Once more, I remembered UPI. It occurred to me that our governor and other politicians, so fond of comparing business to education, would be terrible CEOs, running their corporations into the ground—or bankruptcy court—with their negativism. I began to appreciate my management experience and the corporate emphasis on merit and morale.

I did library research to determine whether what I saw at Oklahoma State and later at Ohio University applied to other institutions across the country. I clipped dozens of articles from publications like *Chronicle of Higher Education,* which reported decreased funding for higher education in many states and increased emphasis on accountability. As noted earlier in my acknowledgements, I also interviewed colleagues at other institutions. Because I am a creative writer and journalist, I often am invited to give presentations at private and public colleges; this gave me a broader perspective as I spoke to professors about other merit systems and morale problems. Soon I began writing about education reform and received more information and support from readers of literary magazines. Thus, while many of my examples in this book are drawn from personal experience at two fine institutions—one my alma mater and the other, my place of employment—I have chosen topics carefully. This is not a book about merit and morale problems in Oklahoma and Ohio but about academic problems that appear to be widespread. Moreover, in the second half of this book, dozens of educators and business and government leaders often substantiate—and sometimes dispute—my stance and opinions.

In sum, the goal of this book is not to accuse any institution but to redirect the education reform debate so that it focuses on administrative accountability and the impact of an inadequate merit system. I maintain that this system (or variations thereof) exists on many campuses and contributes to low productivity and morale. These are the issues that I will raise in this book.

ACADEMIC SOCIALISM

The term has a history. I conceived "academic socialism" in the mid-1980s during the financial crisis at Oklahoma State University but refined the idea while at Ohio University, publishing an essay by that title in the Fall 1992 edition of *The Midwest Quarterly*.

I'll define "academic socialism" by quoting from that piece:"[M]any professors allow their administrators to treat them under a system not unlike socialism: when times are good, so are the five-year plans. When times are bad, everyone is average.

"This is the core of the cancer in the typical American college. Merit and motivation are paradigms lost. Just as a socialist government puts interests of the state before the citizen, *academic socialism* puts the system before the individual. Administrators embrace a philosophy that rewards or punishes across the board, that takes the easiest route, that sells out to industry and forgets tradition, ruining young adults and putting our nation at risk." [1]

I believe our academic system is in need of an overhaul. But unlike authors of other education books promoting similar notions, I will recommend reforms that are not only easily put into place but that also do not require more taxation and funding. They do demand courage and a change in attitude. Moreover, the reforms concern morale and merit rooted in business practice *without surrendering to entrepreneurialism and so jeopardizing educational values.*

Metaphorically, business—as opposed to government—is linked to education. It is time that educators acknowledge this relationship and understand how business methods have evolved in our rapidly changing world (while education, for the most part, has remained stagnant). For instance, few scholars will argue that the university system is patterned after the factory model of the 19th Century. Charles W. Anderson, in his book *Prescribing the Life of the Mind,* bluntly states: "Fundamentally, the America university thinks of itself as a knowledge factory. It was created to rationalize and systematize, in effect to industrialize, the pursuit of knowledge."[2]

As I write, however, fewer than 1 in 12 Americans work in a factory. Automation and computerization have seen to that. Competition has increased because of communications technology, free trade agreements, and better access to global markets. As a result, management practices have also changed, emphasizing quality control and customer service and satisfaction. The old UPI motto— "Get it first, get it fast, get it right"—can apply now to any successful enterprise, Fortune 500 to the corner Kinko's. Undergirding the business world and its bottom line, the profit margin, is a reform that has nothing to do with profit but what executives believe is the means to it: employee morale.

Conversely, education and the state government that funds it have forgotten the importance of the healthy attitude. It amuses me to see administrators and legislators wearing those mini-American flag pins on their lapels and pinafores when often the hammer and sickle would be more appropriate.

I know these are harsh words. They shouldn't apply to all administrators and legislators, of course. But there is also truth in that satire. In a comprehensive review of poor productivity and morale in the old Soviet work force, Guy Standing writes in *International Labor Review*: "Low wages affect work motivation and thus productivity, both directly and by raising labor turnover. Soviet workers are said to rank wages rather low in the factors they look for in a job. For example, a factory study in Zhdanov in 1977 reported that only about 10 per cent of the workers perceived wages to be more important than job content in their choice of job. ... Perhaps more significantly, most workers in a recent survey admitted that they worked below capacity, were dissatisfied with their wages (and were much more inclined to be dissatisfied than were workers in a comparable survey 12 years earlier), and felt that if wages were raised their productivity would increase." [3]

Standing goes on to document the poor Communist economy in which, in essence, every worker had *tenure* along with similar pay checks and low morale. To adjust for those factors, Standing states, many workers coveted "job *status*" [his emphasis]. Finally he mentions the poor evaluation system under which Soviet workers were reviewed; their wages largely were fixed and their benefits guaranteed by the state: "one must question whether an effective, flexible and sophisticated job evaluation scheme is feasible in the Soviet Union at this stage."[4]

The unproductive Soviet worker—with fixed wages and low morale—mirrors the tenured American professor. Typically, he or she knows that they cannot do much to change their salaries under the current merit system and so place a high value on job status: academic title (honorary such as "writer in residence" or earned such as "Regents Professor"), choice committee or teaching assignments, parking (no small matter in academe), and other trappings of rank. When unable to earn enough money or be rewarded fairly via annual reviews, the professor either becomes unproductive ... or moves to a greener campus.

How would such professors have been received in the USSR? The Communist response to low productivity and morale was eerily similar to that of today's education-bashing U.S. legislators. As noted by Yuri Grafsky in his *Soviet Life* article, "Theater of the Economic Absurd": "The Committee for Statistics argues that the main thing is that modern-day workers are not hard-working enough."[5]

Perhaps the politicians here are right and the same is true with the typical tenured professor. But the system that demoralizes him or her is to blame, I posit, and needs to be assessed by analyzing yet another socialist model. In a lament about the failed promises of socialism, and the necessary reform needed to revive those promises, Michael Walzer writes in *The New Republic:* "It would look first to the social infrastructure to reinforce all those networks, fellowships, neighborhoods, service organizations, communities of faith and interest within which people help and support and care for one another. Socialism has often given rise to statist politics, committed to replacing mutual aid with bureaucratic benevolence. That indeed is the record of Communist regimes, except that the bureaucrats never turn out to be benevolent."[6]

Indeed. What we need now more than ever in academe is fellowship, service, faith, help, support, care, mutual aid—all morale-builders; what we don't need are more administrators or benevolent-sounding legislators to fix problems in our infrastructure.

I will try to make that case in the opening chapters of this book. Then I will test my theories and assumptions by sharing the results of surveys to business and education leaders and governor's aides.

CEOs, professors, and aides will make some startling observations.

Here is a sampling:

—"Higher education is really pretty much a business when it comes to the financial aspects of the endeavor. This is particularly true for private institutions. However, most of the academics who teach either can't or won't accept this fact. As a result, there is little concern as to who the real customer is (often the ignored undergraduate) and little attempt to get costs in line with the growth or lack thereof in the economy in general.

"I'll predict that higher education will follow the health industry in being 'helped' by the U.S. government."

(CEO, major U.S. defense contractor)

—"The system of renumeration that creates the best morale gives everyone who does a satisfactory job a small increase, and then allows everyone who believes s/he deserves a merit increase to apply for one. The application is clear and simple. Applications are ranked by peer committees & sent out to the dean, who has a fund for merit and one for equity/compensation. (This system was in place at Old Dominion University in Norfolk when I was there in the mid-80s.)

"Here in Alaska, increases are either across-the-board percentages or market-driven, both of which sleight the humanities and arts, every time. Morale's awful."

(Peggy Shumaker, English professor, Univ. of Alaska-Fairbanks)

—"Individual merit pay provides an incentive for competent teachers— or any employee—to operate independently and to achieve at the expense of his or her peers. There would be no incentive for a good teacher to spend time to assist a poor teacher and make that teacher better. Merit pay should be on a school-wide basis at least to foster a spirit of teamwork, cooperation and mentoring that will ensure every teacher becomes better and that every student benefits. ..."

(Governor's education aide, Wyoming)

After stating my case and presenting ideas about reform, I will make conclusions based on collective views and recommend changes in academe.

NOTES

1 Michael J. Bugeja, "Academic Socialism," *The Midwest Quarterly,* Vol. XXXIV, No. 1, p. 14.
2 Charles W. Anderson, *Prescribing the Life of the Mind,* (Madison, Wis.: Univ. of Wisconsin Press, 1993), p. 23.
3 Guy Standing, "Wages and Work Motivation in the Soviet Labor Market," *International Labor Review,* Vol. 130, No. 2, pp. 240-41.
4 Standing, p. 243.
5 Yuri Grafsky, "Theater of the Economic Absurd," *Soviet Life,* March 1991, p. 29.
6 Michael Walzer, "Socialism Then and Now," *The New Republic,* 6 November 1989, p, 76.

Two

STUDENT SCAPEGOATS

I had one professor last quarter who was terrible. He was cold, unorganized and not helpful. I gained nothing from his class and wasted a lot of time. He didn't care about his students at all. As he put it, 'It doesn't matter, I've got tenure.'

—excerpt from student exit interview

GRADING CRISIS

The student was going to kill herself. She was attractive and in good health, had a caring boyfriend and family—everything a twenty-two-year-old could want—an apartment off campus, a dependable car, a stereo system, and scads of fun-loving friends. But she had some barbiturates and wanted to tell somebody.

So I listened, even though I knew her trouble. This was her fifth year at the university. Tuition had been raised again. Her parents were pressing her to find work, and if she did not perform excellently in two classes, she would lack the grade point to earn a diploma. A student with such a dilemma usually re-enrolls in freshmen courses, and she was doing that—not to learn anything—but to get an easy "A" and increase her overall mark enough to graduate. She had run into a problem, though. No matter how hard she tried, her teachers—with whom she had no quarrel—predicted she would earn average grades once more in each course.

"I should be aceing it all," she complained in my office. "Here I am about to graduate and can't even get an 'A' in beginning reporting." She pleaded with me to help her. "I feel worthless," she said. "How am I ever going to get a job?"

I had no answers that day at Oklahoma State University in 1983, or at least none my student wanted to hear. But I knew when I referred her to counseling that higher education needed evaluation as much as the student did. Her situation was common, and the solution to kill herself, tragic. She was not in school to be enlightened but to earn a grade. Each grade became a deposit or withdrawal from the diploma-bank that promised a good job upon receipt. How could I expect her to understand why one attends a university when no parent or professor seemed to have explained it? For most students, grades are not life or death situations, although their desperation during finals may make it seem so. (In fact, some universities violate fire codes and routinely lock residence hall roofs during examinations because of that fear.) An average grade, such as my student received, can be misperceived as rank failure because she knows all her friends are getting A's and graduating cum laude.

As grade inflation goes, so go the stakes.

On 17 May 1993, The Associated Press cited these statistics:

—43 percent of the grades awarded now at Harvard are A's or A-minuses, compared with 22 percent 20 years earlier.

—35 percent of all grades at Stanford were A's in 1987, the last year for which figures were available.

—40 percent of all grades at Princeton in 1992 were A's, up from 33 percent in 1989.

The AP piece also quoted a Harvard government professor, Harvey C. Mansfield, who said: "Not every student is equally good. It's unfair to the best students to have them mixed up with the not-as-good students or even with the mediocre students." Mansfield might be able to make that claim to the media. Try to do so to a disgruntled advisee in your office, however, and you might be hit with a complaint about your lack of sensitivity.

Students take grades as seriously as professors take parking.

In a satirical *Newsweek* piece, Roberta F. Borkat, an English professor at San Diego State University, proposed a solution to grade-anxiety disorders: "The plan is simplicity itself: at the end of the second week of the semester, all students enrolled in each course will receive a final grade of A. ... Students will be assured of high grade-point averages and an absence of obstacles in their march toward graduation. Professors will be relieved of useless burdens and will have time to pursue their real interests. Universities will have achieved the long-desired goal of molding individual professors into interchangeable parts of a smoothly operating machine."[1]

A "rehabilitated" Borkat adds: "I, too, used to think that knowledge was important and that we should encourage hard work and perseverance. Now I realize that the concept of rewards for merit is elitist and, therefore, wrong in a society that aims for equality in all things. We are a democracy. What could be more democratic than to give exactly the same grade to every single student?"[2]

What could be more *socialistic*? Satire aside, equality was never one of America's strong suits. The Puritan work ethic was.

Nonetheless, Borkat's tongue-in-cheek comments are otherwise revealing; her allusions to the meritless academy, on point.

There are other points to ponder. As part of academic freedom, teachers take for granted the right to evaluate students arbitrarily, with A-work in one class worth only C-work in another. They know that the report card remains a tool—in a few cases, a weapon—to reward or set back a student. However easily or unfairly assigned, a grade was never meant to be an economic indicator. It is part of a merit system that made America great, not only in education, but in every facet of society—from Franklin's penny press to Edison's electric lab.

A society without merit is un-American. So is a classroom. Teachers understand this concept, particularly when it comes to grades. They seldom change them, and shouldn't, even under suicide threats (which represent a more desperate plea for help). A government professor like Harvey C. Mansfield, who has taught for more than 30 years, and an English professor like Roberta F. Borkat, who upholds standards, know this, and their attitudes reinforce basic American ideals. And yet many professors like Mansfield and Borkat allow their administrators to treat them under a system not unlike socialism: when times are good, so are raises and five-year-plans. When times are bad, everyone is lousy.

CASTING BLAME

In 1987, two books—*Cultural Literacy* by E.D. Hirsch, Jr. and *The Closing of The American Mind* by Allan Bloom—rekindled a national debate about education in this country. Since then the book stores have been flooded by texts, explaining what is wrong with the academy and proposing sweeping reforms. The media, seeing an easy story and easier target, has joined the choir of complaints. Not to be left out, but usually last to act, the politicians sensed an easy slogan and easier sell to an overtaxed electorate.

Meanwhile the business community was donating millions to universities in the form of scholarships and endowments. CEOs were relatively unconcerned about their tax-break investments; many of their corporations were *saving* millions by using universities for cheap labor and research, especially in the sciences. But their worry was genuine. Business leaders, by and large a patriotic lot, believe in old-fashioned American merit; upon reading reports about academe, they feared that a decline in standards would affect the quality of entry-level employees and corporate-endowed research.

Hirsch and Bloom had got their attention.

The Hirsch book, known for its 60-plus pages of alphabetized lists comprising "What Literate Americans Should Know," makes a strong case for a common language that augments learning. The Bloom book, an eloquent but often misargued manifesto about America's spiritual malaise, attacks cultural openness as the root cause of a valueless education. Anyone who has read them knows the books are different in content and approach; Hirsch and Bloom should not be lumped together but often are because each work was timely in 1987, distrusted the influence of John Dewey, and acknowledged the importance of Great Books (much to the chagrin of those who would promote diversity). Many current-day scholars and education-bashers would dismiss Hirsch and Bloom, unaware that they are echoing, disputing, debating, and improvising upon Hirsch-Bloom agendas.

These two authors set the parameters for the debate. Subsequent books—some by university officials who possess the power to change the system—do not focus on administrators and the climate that they have created to lessen their managerial responsibilities. For example, this charge by Bloom has gone largely unaddressed: "Our present educational problems cannot seriously be attributed to bad administrators, weakness of will, lack of discipline, lack of money, insufficient attention to the three R's, or any of the other common explanations. ..."[3]

I believe a significant portion of present educational problems can be attributed to bad administrators. When Bloom exonerated them, he helped set the parameters of the debate about reform. The focus then was on the professor, and author Charles J. Sykes spearheaded the assault. His *Profscam: Professors and the Demise of Higher Education* touched off a series of media and legislative inquiries in the early 1990s that continue to this day and that increasingly have been deflected by faculty unions, lobbyists, and university governing boards.

Conveniently, that leaves a scapegoat: the student.

STUDENT MYTHS

For me, 1983 at Oklahoma State University was a pivotal year. I became a full-time assistant professor then, no longer advising the campus newspaper. While my professional newsroom skills may have enhanced my teaching, they did not prepare me for my encounter with the student body. Up until then I associated mostly with hands-on types who wrote, edited, and burned out at *The O'Collegian* newsroom. Now I taught required classes with large enrollments whose majors included advertising, public relations, broadcasting, photography and wildlife science.

I still thought of myself as a UPI manager, not a teacher. One day at the chalkboard, frustrated because my students were taking shortcuts to earn grades, copying notes from each other, cheating on tests, I asked them: "Why is education important in America?"

I put their answers on the board:

—To get a job.

—To put off getting a job.

—To earn money to buy things.

—To learn the latest technology.

—To develop social skills.

—To have an easier life than our parents.

—To be a part of management and not labor.

—To keep one step ahead of the Russians.

I still ask this question in my ethics class. The Reagan-era response about Russia has been replaced by concerns about "empowerment" and "environment" but the other answers essentially are the same. In 1983, only one student who had transferred from the Air Force Academy knew the constitutional reply: *to educate citizens of a republic so that no country or person can take advantage of them.*

Typically, between one and three students out of 90 in my ethics class at Ohio University (also a required course for multiple majors) understand that question. They know that a diploma is not a work permit but a symbol of enlightenment as valuable in our moral development as the pledge of allegiance. The other students are not to blame, however. They genuinely believe that their grade point will get them a job more than their experience or values. They believe that business will be impressed with transcripts that lack any C's, D's, and F's. Our school has selective admissions, attracting the best and brightest to our program—which might, in part, explain their high grades; however, lesser students cheat on tests and take shortcuts because of peer pressure, they tell me in exit interviews (more on that later). If everyone earns an A or a B, and more than 50 percent of the students in my College do, then everyone can secure a job upon graduation.

Question: Could such a myth about grades (everyone is equal) have come from administrators who promote across-the-board "excellence" to regents and alumni?

Question: Could such a myth about the role of education (to secure employment) have come from "patriotic" legislators who appeal to tuition-paying voter-parents?

Students are not naive. Their lives are complex by the time they take their seats in freshman composition. Typically, they enter college without much of a childhood, having dealt already with such issues as divorce, drugs, violence, suicide, and AIDS. Some men bring weapons to class. Some women already have been raped. Yet the current climate in academe most likely will deprive students of the one remaining legacy of selfhood: enlightenment.

Critics of the current generation too often underestimate its intellectual yearning. They place blame where it does not belong. A colleague in the sociology department, discussing the woes of freshmen advising, commiserated recently with me. "These days," he said, "you don't have to convince the students about the value of education, but the parents. Before they invest in tuition, they want to know the rate of return. What type of job will their child get with a particular degree? What salary?"

Statistics bear out his observations. In a report by the Public Agenda Foundation for the California Higher Education Policy Center, surveys revealed that 76 percent of Californians "endorse the view that high school graduates should go on to college because in the long run they'll have better job prospects."[4] Here is a quote from a San Jose respondent that sums up the general consensus: "The more education the more you have a chance to get a job." Another San Jose respondent added, "If I am going to be an accountant, what do I care what someone did in ancient Egypt?"

California, it turns out, reflects U.S. attitudes about higher education.

The Public Agenda Foundation also conducted a national survey. It reported that nearly eight out of ten Americans, or 79 percent, are convinced that high school graduates should go to college because they will have better job opportunities.[5]

Students believe this by the time they become seniors; everyone else at home and at school reinforces the idea. The bachelor's degree is a license to practice life at the middle class level. So most students openly accept their meritless milieu. When it comes to grades, they are content to judge themselves by tenths of a percentage point. If a student graduates with an overall GPA of 3.1 on a 4.0 scale, peers know that this is average "C" work. The person with a 3.8 or above overall GPA is really excellent, they realize, and their future employers will recognize this even if their parents don't.

In sum, most upperclassmen not only accept grade inflation. They perpetuate it.

STUDENT EVALUATIONS

Students are easy graders. In my magazine writing workshop I let them grade each other on the editing portion of the class, which represents 25 percent of the total grade. I used to trust that my students read each other's copy before workshop so that we could critique the article or essay as a group. Then I learned that they showed up for class unprepared and were taking cues from me and winging it, not even reading stories because they weren't being graded on that component.

Products of academic socialism, they have learned from their professors to do only what is required.

Worse, no student had complained. (Each spends $25 photocopying his or her manuscript for the class for critique purposes, so you would think the students—especially the environmentalists—would be angered at the waste of money and paper.) I discovered the practice one day when I decided not to give cues but to listen to what students had to say about a particularly controversial piece. I stared at my class for 10 minutes as they quickly paged through the essay, speed-reading. The rest of the quarter I policed their edits, reviewing each copy before class, a time-consuming and presumably unnecessary chore in a seminar format that assumes people have opinions.

One day a student called me "anal."

By the next quarter, I was rehabilitated. I decided to forfeit one-quarter of the grade and rely on peer pressure, requiring students to read and edit copy, tightening and correcting language and suggesting thematic or other changes in each essay. Students are asked to make overall comments about the piece on the back of the last page and then sign it. When copies of the essay are returned to the author, he or she must evaluate the editing effort of each classmate and assign a grade from 0 to 100. Grading sheets are handed in to me at the end of the term so that I can calculate averages for each student.

It worked. Now students show up prepared to critique. They have opinions, too. They put a fair amount of effort into their critiques and reward each other with high grades.

Here are the final averaged grades for each student based on peer evaluation in my most recent class:

Student #1 A-	Student #8 A-
Student #2 A	Student #9 A-
Student #3 A-	Student #10 A
Student #4 A	Student #11 A-
Student #5 B+	Student #12 B+
Student #6 A	Student #13 A
Student #7 A	Student #14 B

A few professors have correlated my grading practices with my popularity as a teacher. Typically, on teacher evaluations, all 14 to 16 students enrolled in a writing workshop will give me perfect scores of 5.0. Perhaps I am no longer as "anal" as some of my colleagues want me to be. While it is popular in academe to come out against grade inflation, I don't hear too many professors in the Communications College at Ohio University complain about their similarly inflated scores on teaching evaluations.

Here are the mean figures for the Journalism School and College (comprising five communications schools) accompanying questions of the most recent teacher evaluation:

1. The teacher was enthusiastic about the subject matter.
    Journalism: 4.45   College: 4.47
2. The teacher was knowledgeable about the subject matter.
    Journalism: 4.54   College: 4.56
3. The teacher evaluates students fairly.
    Journalism: 4.21   College: 4.04
4. I could get help from this teacher.
    Journalism: 4.12   College: 4.09
5. I felt I had the opportunity to participate.
    Journalism: 4.27   College: 4.32
6. The teacher followed the syllabus.
    Journalism: 4.31   College: 4.26
7. I'd recommend this teacher to other students.
    Journalism: 4.20   College: 4.12
8. I learned a lot in this course.
    Journalism: 4.06   College: 3.99
9. The course encouraged me to think.
    Journalism: 3.97   College: 3.96
10. I understood what was expected of me.
    Journalism: 4.15   College: 4.03
11. The goals of the course are clear.
    Journalism: 4.18   College: 4.04
12. The course is valuable.
    Journalism: 4.21   College: 4.11
13. The course is relevant to my life/career.
    Journalism: 4.03   College: 4.00
14. I'd recommend this course to other students.
    Journalism: 4.09   College: 3.97

Like my students, I, too, evaluate my teaching effectiveness by tenths and hundreds of a percentage point.

Now compare average grades that students gave each other in my workshop, with average grades that all journalism students gave departmental teachers, changed to letters instead of mean scores:

Student #1 A-	Question #1 A
Student #2 A	Question #2 A
Student #3 A-	Question #3 A-
Student #4 A	Question #4 A-
Student #5 B+	Question #5 A-
Student #6 A	Question #6 A
Student #7 A	Question #7 A-
Student #8 A-	Question #8 A-
Student #9 A-	Question #9 B+
Student #10 A	Question #10 A-
Student #11 A-	Question #11 A-
Student #12 B+	Question #12 A-
Student #13 A	Question #13 A-
Student #14 B	Question #14 A-
Final Grade A-	Final Grade A-

Everyone is nearly excellent, and the "nearly" allows everyone enough room to figure out who is *really* excellent ... and who isn't.

EXIT INTERVIEWS

You don't have to convince personnel managers that exit interviews provide a wealth of information. Employees who leave a company willingly or under duress have candid things to say that might help executives build morale, reward merit, or enhance the quality of the work environment and/or product.

I no longer rely much on student evaluations to gauge my performance. Instead I ask seniors when they graduate to give me exit interviews. Such interviews prepared me in part for the issues probed in this book. Here is an abbreviated one from one of my workshop writers who works now at a trade magazine in New York City:

June 1993
Dear Dr. Bugeja:
I think the college atmosphere is very distracting. I don't mean just the partying, but the pressure of it all as well. I feel like I have to excel at what I am doing because if I don't I'm wasting money. It shouldn't be like that. Instead, I think an atmosphere should be created where the pressure to excel is there, but that also says "knowledge is its own excuse for being." I guess that this country just doesn't feel that way because everyone is so eager for success and wealth. Before I came to college here I wanted to gain knowledge just because I wanted to know. I took classes that I thought would be interesting, because I wanted to know about lots of different things. But I got to the point where I chose classes because I thought that I'd get a good grade in them. I've avoided classes that sounded interesting because I didn't want to hurt my GPA. I hate it that I think like this, and I don't know why my attitude changed to this. I don't want to be a lazy person who takes the easy way out, but it's hard not to be that way when I keep getting told that my GPA is everything, and who cares if I'm gaining anything from the class as long as it's easy? ...

I had one professor last quarter who was terrible. He was cold, unorganized and not helpful. I gained nothing from his class and wasted a lot of time. He didn't care about his students at all. As he put it, "It doesn't matter, I've got tenure."

That attitude makes me sick. What is he being paid for? He certainly doesn't deserve it. And how did he even get tenure? People like that shouldn't be allowed to teach, especially in college.

I have had some good classes, and I probably should mention that. I guess I was just expecting more.
Sincerely,
Heidi Sacko

I don't have to elaborate much on the points and themes of this student's exit interview. She feels pressured by the job emphasis of academe and thinks that she has to sacrifice her hunger for knowledge. Like her peers, she measures her job potential by her GPA and avoids classes that might hurt it. She's not sure when, why, and how her attitude changed about education, but she is sure that she didn't always feel this way. Finally, she probably had 40 tenured professors during her four years at OU but remembers the bad teacher who waved his lifetime *employment*—the very thing on her mind—in her face. In her defense I can say that she is too hard on herself, as most conscientious students are in such interviews, pondering the chance of having a second chance in academe. At this writing she is applying to graduate school after six months in the work force. Her journalism skills are superior—getting a choice magazine job in Manhattan isn't easy—but she is still hungry for knowledge and has decided to brave academe again, pursuing a master's degree in history. It seems that we prepared an intelligent woman to perform well in the business world but failed to satisfy her mind. So she is leaving the business world. Had we focused more on her mind, and less on GPAs and jobs, perhaps her magazine would have a future executive instead of a vacancy. Worse, as more students like her return to graduate school because their undergraduate work did not sate their hunger for knowledge, perhaps higher education surveys in the year 2020 will bemoan the fact that a master's degree is needed to enhance one's job prospects.

As educational values decline, minimum degree requirements increase.

NOTES

1 Roberta F. Borkat, "A Liberating Curriculum," *Newsweek*, 12 April 1993, p. 11.
2 Borkat, p. 11.
3 Allan Bloom, *The Closing of the American Mind* (New York: Simon and Schuster, 1987), p. 312.
4 John Immerwahr with Steve Farkas, *The Closing Gateway: Californians Consider Their Education System,* Public Agenda Foundation, September 1993, p. 1.
5 Immerwahr and Farkas, p. 19.

Three

BAD ATTITUDES

Administrators should bolster morale when forced to make cutbacks by cutting administrators. Doing so would be a guaranteed morale-bolsterer.

Professor, Southwest State University, Marshall, Minnesota

MORALE BUSTERS

"Our universities aren't any better off than the people who put money in the basket," Ohio Governor George Voinovich was quoted as saying in *Columbus Dispatch* in the summer of 1993. He was right. Voinovich had helped Ohio come out of the recession, luring businesses to the state and improving the unemployment rate. But many people were still suffering. After 2 1/2 years in office, Voinovich had earned a reputation as an education-buster, cutting university allocations repeatedly. Every three months or so we would hear about another shortfall and brace ourselves for another gubernatorial attack. The higher the shortfall, the lower our morale. By July 1993, however, the Legislature was restoring some funding. Nonetheless, the governor was siding with voters. "Students and their families have been clobbered by increases in tuition in the past several years," he said in the article, neglecting to mention the policies in Columbus that caused the hikes. Then he appealed to the private sector, as also was his habit, emphasizing that education must learn to do as business has done: *More with less.*[1]

Voinovich, an alumnus of Ohio University and former mayor of Cleveland, should not be singled out. He is not the first nor the last nor the only governor using higher education as a scapegoat. If the budget were healthy, he probably would be in Asia making trade agreements and encouraging ambassadors to continue sending their best and brightest to our campuses, some of the finest in the world.

But the economy in Ohio was not good in the early 1990s, so Voinovich wanted to make education accountable.

In the last election in Ohio, most educators I know voted for his benevolent-sounding Democratic rival, Anthony Celebrezze. We were fooling ourselves, behaving like socialists who would rather put their faith in a sympathetic leader than any energy in our cause. Chances are Celebrezze would have disappointed educators, too. Like Voinovich, he would have had to choose between cutting welfare or education; unlike him, he would have said a kind word at the chopping block before he hefted the axe. (In truth, that would have helped our morale.) Voinovich, however, has found it easier to browbeat a professor in the name of a hungry child in Appalachia or Dayton. He decided that the safest political response was to cut the higher education allotment, knowing that university regents would raise tuition. Then he could appeal to unemployed over-taxed voters, direct their complaints at professors by repeating old arguments about tenure as lifetime employment, and blame education for not being as efficient as business. If Voinovich stands out, perhaps it was in the passion with which he expressed these tired strategies. He may actually have believed them.

Our governor apparently believed that he was Ohio's CEO and felt that this is how CEOs in the real world operate during budgetary crises. The only thing that Voinovich may have proved, however, was that he associated with business executives after hours, when they usually complain about the work force. In the board room they make tough decisions, as Voinovich did in the statehouse, knowing that they will be putting people out of work and the economy into recession. Conversely, many CEOs condone policies to bolster morale and reward remaining employees who, in truth, will be doing more with less.

Cassandra Reese, a colleague of mine in the Journalism School and former executive of Kraft USA, notes that CEOs are particularly attuned to concerns about morale. "I know businesses that cut staff and then give raises to the rest of the employees," she adds, "knowing that they will be working twice as hard." At United Press International, we lacked money for such incentives during downholds, but managers did what we could: praise, retain, conquer.

In the summer of 1993, educators didn't view Voinovich as a businessman. Soon they would get raises for the first time in two years. But they had their own axes to grind. They thought of Voinovich as an unpopular provost whose support was eroding. The governor's "passion of complaint" swept through academe and afflicted the morale of productive professors.

In the winter of 1991, a dark time in Ohio, Roy Flannagan, English professor and editor of the esteemed *Milton Quarterly*, wrote a letter to Voinovich. Flannagan was one of only a few professors who took on the governor early in his assault on the academy. Here is an abbreviated version of his letter:

February 1991
Dear Governor Voinovich:

Several news items that appeared in our local Athens newspaper have upset the Ohio University community (20,000+) a great deal. First, your state government has announced major cuts in the budget for higher education. ... At the same time your government has announced [these cuts], it has announced substantial raises in salary for your cabinet members and for yourself. ... Feathering the nest of your administration [is] especially offensive.

Several of the state legislators and administrators quoted in the same series of news items implied that the state of Ohio is supporting professors who teach little and are "getting paid to write books." The implication is that professors such as myself do not serve students by conducting research, keeping up with current states of knowledge or publishing our own discoveries. Another implication is that we do very little real work. As someone whose average work day begins at five or six AM and ends about eleven PM, and continues at that schedule through the weekend, I resent being told that I do not work hard enough for my students or for the state of Ohio. ... It is an essential part of the job of professors and teachers in general that we take our work home with us, in that we grade papers, we prepare course work and we conduct research that will lead to our being better prepared ... when we do lecture in class. In addition to preparing for class, we are expected to be good citizens of the University community, serving on administrative committees in and outside of our departments, serving on Faculty Senate, preparing and writing grants to bring money into the University. ... If we take on the additional scholarly duties expected of every college professor, we may do something like edit a journal in our "spare time," as I do ... [f]or no additional salary or reward.

There are many other things taken for granted of college professors and teachers in general. We are expected always to have time to talk to our students, we are expected to come to classes when we are ill (taking any amount of sick leave is rare among college professors) and we are expected to serve our students and University in the off-hours, as when I might attend a study session for students the night before a test or serve on the Faculty Senate during the hours when I normally eat dinner. Certainly there are lazy college professors who take their tenure as an excuse to do as little as possible, just as there are lazy state officials or lazy janitors, but most of us work very hard for salaries that do not measure up to professional salaries outside the academic community. Though we have been as carefully educated as lawyers, for instance, our average salary after ten years of service might still be less than that of an average beginning lawyer, even though our hours of service might add up to more per week. ...

Now is not the time for government officials to pay themselves more and take away from education, using professors as whipping posts for any state-wide fiscal irresponsibility. ... To cut our budgets further would send the best candidates for teaching jobs to other states and demoralize those within the Ohio system.

Sincerely,

Roy Flannagan

I let more than two years elapse before getting in touch with Flannagan again in the summer of 1993. The worst part of the recession had ended, and I wanted to see if the feelings that he expressed in his letter to Voinovich had changed in the interim. I told Flannagan that I was writing a book, focusing in part on business methods pertaining to merit and morale. "Speaking of business," Flannagan said, "how many professors at OU have either begun buying cheap real estate when they first come to Athens in order to supplement a not-very-good income with that from student rentals? I ran an extra business for eight years to supplement my income while two of my children were in college. Keeping up University professors' morale may often depend on moonlighting, just as with high-school teachers' morale.

"So, in order to avoid despair," he continued, "I try to consider my lot the way a state legislator does, as only nine months of *real* work, and I try to see my time in the classroom as grossly overpaid, and I forget to add in my time editing or writing letters or going to conferences or polishing papers, because all that isn't *real* work and it certainly should not be *paid* work." Flannagan said that he is not bitter; nonetheless, he added: "But I am starting to think like a state legislator and a union worker on slow-down."

I know what Flannagan means. The complaints out of Columbus against academia had taken their toll, as they had earlier in my academic career in Oklahoma. I didn't own a small-business to keep up my morale, but adjusted my schedule accordingly. I couldn't become less effective as a teacher or less productive as a writer nor did I want to take out frustrations on colleagues or students. However, I did stop speaking in the evenings to student groups, cut back on independent studies (which, at many universities, go unpaid), and said "no" to service assignments like planning banquets and award ceremonies. I still put in a 10-hour day, on average, doing many of the tasks that Flannagan mentions in his letter. But I got up earlier to come home at a decent hour, spending more time with my children. My daughter and new son lifted my spirits so that I could face another day in academe and be enthusiastic about writing and journalism in the classroom.

Other professors at the university did less. Unable to keep up their morale, they admit anonymously that they refused committee assignments, cut back on class requirements (the number of papers, tests, and the like), and reduced office hours. Why not? Administrators were telling us in faculty meetings about state crackdowns; phone records were being analyzed by state auditors for personal calls; and any research, like writing an essay for a well-paying journal like *TriQuarterly*, was deemed personal and so was to be done on one's time. Although few audits were done and no procedures were in place to check the nature of research, Voinovich had succeeded in making many professors feel that they were under personal investigation.

The more accountable the governor made us feel, the less we did. Finally my own School, once known for its good humor and camaraderie, began to embrace the "rule" of the modern university, described by Charles W. Anderson in his book *Prescribing the Life of*

the Mind: "I'll let you alone if you let me alone."[2]
We started to brood.

MISSING PROFESSORS

In the early 1990s, the media wondered about the whereabouts of the missing professor. Almost all of us were in our offices but a few were on the lam. Reporters found them at likely places, such as at home gardening, and at unlikely ones, such as at nudist colonies. Politicians felt vindicated and so bore down harder on unethical professors. One of the most stinging indictments, however, did not come from a journalist or lawmaker but from one of our own.

Milton Greenberg, the former provost of American University, published "Accounting for Faculty Members' Time" in the 20 October 1993 *Chronicle of Higher Education.* Greenberg essentially believes that professors work on a volunteer basis. Anyone interested in accountability should read his essay. These excerpts are but a fraction of the sins documented therein: "Activities related to teaching generally are viewed as optional or as a matter of professional discretion—in other words, voluntary. These include arriving on time, teaching the entire scheduled time, requiring a sufficient number of papers or examinations to assess what students have learned, and holding regular office hours. Except for those office hours, contact with students outside of the classroom also has become almost totally voluntary. ... Faculty members' service obligations are the most voluntary of all. In performing community service, faculty members frequently feel little of the professional pride or peer pressure that may attend teaching or scholarship. They know that they are not really going to be evaluated based on their service activities. When asked to serve on a committee, one can always claim other commitments. If one chooses to serve, there is no serious requirement for attendance, much less active participation. ... When presidents or deans call meetings of their entire faculties, they are exultant if nearly half the faculty shows up."[3]

Greenberg feels that the "voluntary" work ethic of academe can be fixed with proper evaluation methods and appropriate rewards. Moreover, Greenberg recommends "rigorous and thorough *peer* judgment" (my italics); it would seem that he is reluctant to demand that administrators evaluate professors as executives do employees in the business world.

Many of Greenberg's accusations are true, although more for tenured than untenured faculty. And as we shall see in the next chapter, his observation about professors knowing that they will not be evaluated on service is on point. But there are other spins on the litany of sins in this essay, as any professor knows. Try starting a class a few minutes early or keeping students a few minutes late, and some students will complain or storm out. As enrollments increase to 100 students in so-called · "seminars," some professors do cut down on written assignments and tests. In an era of political correctness, the easiest way to lose respect (not to mention tenure) is to associate with undergraduates after hours. And as for attending meetings called by deans, provosts, or presidents, many professors don't show up because, in a word, they believe they have heard it all before. They anticipate the next administrative speech with the fervor of Soviet citizens watching a government channel.

Ambitious lawmakers will read Greenberg's essay and make more statements that result in lower morale and more volunteerism in academe, jeopardizing tenure and outside research interests. It is easier and safer, politically, to attack a professor than an administrator who might have powerful friends in the country club.

Robert V. Iosue, retired president of York College in Pennsylvania, responded to Greenberg's essay pointedly with a letter in the 17 November 1993 *Chronicle*: "Mr. Greenberg, you were the provost at American University for 13 years, long enough to do something about a condition that is as deplorable at your institution as it is at many large institutions, as well as many of our smaller more elite colleges. As provost you were in a position to address the problem and, over time, bring about needed change. Perhaps complaisant leadership, which recognizes the self-interest of faculty, is more to blame. ... "

I cannot speak about the accountability of Milton Greenberg, who is probably more productive than the typical professor at his institution. Neither do I know his record as provost. Yet it is common knowledge among the professoriate that too many administrators fail to motivate teachers, avoiding confrontations with them at all costs and allowing the sins that Greenberg cites to ruin an academic unit. Then, faced with feuds that cannot heal or accreditation problems that will not go away, these academic socialists blame faculty and step down, becoming tenured professors and committing many of the same offenses, but often at higher cost, taking with them the inflated salaries of their old administrative posts.

THE DEMERIT SYSTEM

We all associate the term "demerit" with education, usually given in grade school to a pupil who has committed an offense. Most elementary teachers or principals would reward a child who takes on extra work; few would punish the child if, for some reason, he or she couldn't complete the unrequired assignment.

In higher education, they punish. Typically an administrator will hint at unspoken rewards if a professor takes on an extra task. (At Oklahoma State University, I directed the Southwest Cultural Heritage Festival, an arts and humanities conference featuring about 40 speakers and a nightmare to schedule, fund, and manage). In any case, the unrequired task usually relates to service, such as agreeing to be part of a Speakers Bureau and traveling to alumni groups across the state; or an unpopular activity, hosting "Research Day" and inviting speakers to campus; or a solicitation, writing a diversity grant because one is a person of color and the administrator isn't.

Something may go wrong. The main speaker for the festival might miss his plane or cancel. An assistant professor might seem dangerously liberal or conservative to a "cherished" alum (who donates money). A junior professor with ambition but no tenure might threaten a senior professor by being enthusiastic about research. The diversity grant is denied. Any of these outcomes beyond the control of the professor in question can be used against him or her during evaluations.

Professors know how to circumvent the demerit system. They accept the risks until tenure is granted and then say "no," reducing the number of opportunities to fail and be held accountable. It is the way some professors keep up their morale.

So-called productive professors do not catch on as quickly, however.

One day in the fall of 1991, I was making my way to the parking lot when I bumped into my dean Paul Nelson. We have a common background; I covered the Dakotas as a reporter for UPI and my wife Diane is from East River in South Dakota, not far from the western Minnesota border where Nelson was reared. Nelson has a sense of humor and sharp wit that I admire. But on this day he was all business, asking me to write a grant to design a course that would serve the university. I listened and agreed.

Although it was close to 5 p.m., I doubled back to my office and banged out the grant according to the guidelines that he had given me. The task went quickly. That evening I put the grant proposal in an envelope so that Nelson would get it the next day in campus mail.

. A few months later, the grant was approved. I was appointed project director to design a course featuring the talents of award-winning professors in the Communications College. I compiled and wrote a report and several of us gathered for a day in a seminar, in which we conceived "Culture and Communication 201." We each got stipends that averaged about $1000 for books and supplies and our time but we would teach without any compensation other than "comp time." If we taught the class a certain number of quarters, we could eliminate one class from our regular schedule in a future quarter. Not a wonderful deal, but we took it willingly.

We wanted to showboat, donating our time in the evenings to share what we loved with students and perhaps attract the brightest nonmajors to our College. For example, Terry Eiler of the Visual Communications School was excited about the course because he could show slides of Native Americans and illustrate how they were stereotyped via photography through the years. To share his set of slides would be a break from the technical and professional aspects of his usual teaching load. As he put it at the seminar, "I just want to show up and do my thing."

This was not an unreasonable request. In fact, I think the best teachers show up and "do their things"—slang for "passion" or "enthusiasm." Students who witness this often are moved to explore their own passions and enthusiasms and mimic their mentors.

All of us in Culture and Communication had credentials. Three of us had won major teaching awards and boasted the highest student evaluations in our disciplines. Surely the course would go off as planned, I assumed.

I was wrong. Professors may not undergo rigorous and thorough peer review when evaluated for merit raises, but their courses do. First one must clear a proposal with the curriculum committee in a department or school. Then it goes to another committee at the College level. Finally the course is evaluated at the university level. At each stage, recommendations are made and amendments required. Innovative proposals usually are watered down so that they come out of committee looking like the last proposal.

Typically, panel members want to know if the content of a course will infringe on their territories or otherwise undermine academic theories or agendas. In our case, we lacked a textbook so we could assign readings; we had no attendance policies and did not use multiple choice examinations that could be graded by computer. Some of us used our own research for lectures and didn't take roll because students came enthusiastically to hear us; they couldn't skip class and read the text. The ones who did skip usually failed because essay/analysis questions on exams were based on lectures.

All this was going to be homogenized, socialist style.

I realized that I was in trouble. The University committee required amendments that would make our innovative course appear like other survey courses. If I agreed, I knew the talented professors involved in the course would be asked to teach it in a manner that they had long since deemed ineffective. If I didn't revise the course, I would be wasting tax money and creating problems for myself via the demerit system.

I agreed to the revisions. No one wanted to pilot the sinking ship and be the main professor, responsible for seating charts, computer-gradable exams, reading assignments, and scheduling. We had wanted to emphasize experiential learning and innovative exams that encouraged students to think about the impact of media on society. For example, a student would read—"Blacks are biologically superior to whites when it comes to sports"—and record his or her reaction to the statement. A student who had attended the lectures would recognize the stereotyping. In any case, the professor would review responses the next day in class and determine how mass media had influenced the attitudes of students, sparking debate and discussion.

Instead we would be taking roll, assigning boring ("safe") textbook readings for quizzes and submitting what many of us disdained: true/false questions.

Judith Lee, an untenured assistant professor at the time, was chosen to lead the course. In retrospect, her nomination was unfair on many counts: Lee was not an original member of the seminar group that designed the class and now she would be telling tenured professors what, how, and when to do it. Lee, a member of the School of Interpersonal Communications, knew what she was in for as captain of our Titanic. She tried to motivate us by asking Paul Nelson to donate an additional $200 to each guest professor for more books and supplies. (Discouraged, I donated my $200 along with the remaining project-director money to the Journalism Department, so we could buy paper and pay telephone bills, offsetting the governor's budget cut that year.)

As predicted, the course bombed.

Paul Nelson was bemused. "If the worst five professors taught this class," he told me, "instead of the best five, we probably would have had better student evaluations."

I requested the student evaluations to try to determine what had happened, but these documents—usually featuring inflated scores as illustrated in Chapter Two—were so low that Judith Lee's director Sue DeWine hesitated to let guest teachers see them, because she was worried about morale (good thing, too).

DeWine told me that sharing the evaluations would be nonproductive because students found the class "boring and not helpful."

She elaborated in a memo: "Student comments like, 'After taking this class I would never recommend majoring in this field' lead me to conclude that the class simply did not work. Probably the variety of instructors and the lack of consistency in having a single instructor made it difficult to identify with the class. We chose some of the very best instructors. I think the format didn't work."

The class was killed, and professors were relieved.

Judith Lee shared some of my frustrations. She said in a long letter that she felt "charged with a very large responsibility for an important course that [she] had little role in conceptualizing. I am very keen on experiential learning, as you well know, and would have liked to see that aspect of the original proposal maintained. And I share your belief that the system for approving new courses is inherently conservative."

But Lee cited other reasons for the demise of the class:
—[D]espite enormous effort on the part of six faculty members ... the students seemed to get so little out of it. And indeed, the class attracted a group of students who, through no fault of their own, really wanted to be somewhere other than Communications 201. ...
—[T]he class had less of an intellectual rationale than an administrative and financial one. ...

There is truth here, too. Although I didn't know it when approached to write my grant, I learned that administrators were considering withholding a faculty position in Journalism because, they felt, the College of Communication was not serving the entire university adequately with general offerings. All the while I had thought administrators were interested in my research in culture and communications. Typical of most professors, I knew nothing about the politics behind the academic curtain.

I should have known better than to take on extra work.

Many professors *do* know better. They realize that once they have tenure, any contribution above and beyond the call of duty can be used against them. This is part of the demerit system that leads to volunteerism in academe. In our case, professors who taught Culture and Communication weren't punished. Our dean understood the forces that caused the class to fail—indeed, he had removed obstacles to get the stalled course out of committee—and later even acknowledged morale problems and so regained trust.

In the end my wife said to me, "I don't know why you get yourself involved in these things." I knew what she meant. Tenured, I could say "no" to such projects. I didn't need to volunteer. I needed to survive in a socialist system that features more routes to punishment than reward.

LIFETIME EMPLOYMENT

When Charles W. Anderson talks about the mission of academe as *Prescribing the Life of the Mind,* the title of his 1993 book, one has to wonder if he is referring to Prozac. There is no question that assistant and associate professors who lack tenure do the bulk of the everyday work at most institutions, as they do in business. The reporter on probation labors twice as long as one who isn't on probation because he or she has yet to prove his or her worth to the company. Likewise the reporter works longer hours than the copy desk editor because he or she wants to win a beat or scoop a competitor. The publisher usually works least. The same holds true for other businesses. A shoe salesperson who is on probation works harder than one who isn't, the successful salesperson works harder than the district manager, and so on upward to the CEO. There are two important distinctions, however, between the academic and business worlds: the latter is driven by merit and morale and bosses usually accept blame when the buck, or lack thereof, stops at their desks.

When professors become demoralized, tenure becomes suspect.

Administrators claim that they look for ways to improve morale. They seek advice that is token at best, because little or no money exists to make the necessary impact on education. So proposals like these evolve: the brown-bag lunch during which faculty may air gripes, the student symposium during which superior papers may be presented, the award ceremony during which budget-saving ideas may be honored with a little cash, the orientation during which newcomers may be advised about how to meet tenure.

All nice, all ineffective.

Professors eventually realize this and become cynical. Fact is, morale is contagious. The teacher carries it to class with lecture notes, and students either glow or suffer from it. However, there is no place in the university for glaring non-productivity, bad attitude, departmental bickering or cliques. Yet many administrators tolerate incompetents in a department and ignore feuds that consume faculty and students. They do so, they say, because of tenure.

Imagine if business managers felt this way. At United Press International, we had deadwood, as all companies do. Some employees with seniority knew that we couldn't fire them because we would have to pay out thousands in severance pay and unemployment benefits. There was the threat of union involvement, too. This created a kind of tenure system that forced managers to motivate employees or make life difficult for them via reassignments.

Increasingly in today's business world, executives are trying to motivate instead of punish employees. In a recent *Business Week* article that discusses corporate "lesson plans" and morale-builders, a Bell Atlantic executive states, "If you worked here for five years and you didn't steal anything, then you pretty much had a job for life."[4] Companies now emphasize quality and service. Consequently, businesses like Bell Atlantic encourage employees to express themselves and make recommendations to enhance the work environment.

In business, the number of employees who abuse the system is relatively small. The same applies to professors who abuse tenure. Even professors who refuse to attend an administrator's faculty meeting or serve on his or her committee or reduce office hours still contribute to academe. Typically they work on lectures, grading, advising, consulting, researching, writing, directing theses and dissertations, composing letters of recommendation for students, and doing the other dozen or so chores that make for a 40-hour week. The number of professors who openly abuse tenure is about 2 or 3 percent.[5]

Yet these are usually the professors whom students and executives remember and whom administrators, alas, overlook. Teachers know that one or two unruly students can ruin an entire class, and administrators know that one or two tenure-abusing professors can ruin an entire unit's image. The difference is that most teachers feel obliged to discipline or motivate unruly students whereas many administrators refuse to accept that responsibility.

David Dary, director of the Journalism School at Oklahoma University, wants administrators to live up to their managerial obligations. This is crucial, he says, in an era of accountability.

"They (administrators) will have no choice but to improve faculty productivity either by trying to change the academic behavior of the non-performing professors or to replace them with professors who will perform."

Changing the behavior of non-performers will occur if "the administrator is strong, determined, and has the support of administrators higher in the pecking order," Dary adds.

In another controversial essay, "What It Takes for Professors to Get Themselves Fired," Jacob Neusner, a distinguished professor from the University of South Florida, writes about a tenured professor who had taken two full-time jobs at different universities and got canned from both. That is what it takes to get fired, Neusner maintains (despite the fact that many universities complicate this issue by encouraging full-time faculty to teach on an overload basis at branch campuses). He recounts other types of academic sins: a disgruntled professor who refused to attend meetings or speak to anyone, a chairman who barred some professors from meetings because other professors didn't like them, a president who didn't answer letters from a chairman he found bothersome.

Neusner states: "Professors who miss classes don't get fired. Professors who come to classes unprepared don't get fired. Professors who don't hold office hours for students, who don't even talk to colleagues from one month to the next, don't get fired. Unless budget problems intervene, everyone gets across-the-board raises every year, no matter what they do—or more to the point—no matter what they don't do."[6]

Neusner also criticizes the ethics of the professor in question who took two posts in different states and didn't inform his deans (but fulfilled his obligations). In the business world, Neusner adds, "you get fired for not doing your job. But you don't get fired for doing two jobs ... if you do both of them well."

One can certainly work at McDonald's in the morning and drive a cab in the evening, as long as one doesn't slack off. White-collar jobs are more demanding. Most employees would not think of working in the same capacity for two similar businesses (essentially what the fired professor did). An employee who did likewise would be fired from both jobs. In the media, some reporters cannot even write for the city or regional magazine or do public relations in their off-hours or get involved with organizations that might cause conflicts of interest. I doubt that Bell Atlantic would condone a manager working at night for

Sprint.

But this is not Neusner's real point. He believes that professors have enough time on their hands to *succeed* at two jobs, letting out what he calls academe's "dirty little secret."

Dary, at Oklahoma University, calls it "the unmentionable myth of academe." He adds, "There are many professors who are scholars and fine teachers, and who meet their responsibilities by inspiring their students in the free pursuit of learning and independence of mind while holding before them the highest scholarly and professional standards. But most of the non-performers do not. They fail to admit that everyone is responsible to someone.

"Whether or not administrators will succeed in improving faculty productivity may well determine the future support of taxpayers who pay the bills in public institutions," Dary concludes.

I foresee another scenario. If administrators fail to address morale problems that cause non-productivity, blaming tenure instead of their management styles, tenure will be abolished—along with academic freedom—and abuses will remain. Critics who focus exclusively on tenure as the root problem in academe are looking for a quick fix and overlooking administrative accountability. Remember that I am invoking tenure and academic freedom now to criticize the system of higher education and earlier, even the governor of my state. The gutsy UPI of old would not tolerate such behavior. I doubt any company would. The news media, so quick to support the First Amendment, generally is well-behaved when publishers and owners tell reporters not to expose businesses that also advertise in their outlets. Jacob Neusner might know how difficult it is to fire a professor but forgets how easy it can be in business when an employee exposes the boss or the boss's friends.

Worse, if academic socialism remains and tenure goes, so too will go the most productive faculty. Many will be fired by administrators who resent reformist, diverse, or nontraditional ideas. Others will be sacrificed by their own peers to maintain a philosophy or worse, the status quo.

The historical and often cited reason for tenure still holds: academic freedom. Imagine if we removed rights from our own U.S. Bill of Rights, the Fifth Amendment say, because most of the defendants who take it also abuse it. Law enforcement might like that idea because district attorneys wouldn't have to work so hard to make a case against criminals. But innocent people would suffer. Similarly, tenure must be retained until the academic socialist system is changed to reflect merit. The burden is on administrators. If they don't take the lead to increase morale and with it productivity, the best professors will leave academe for jobs in the business world, where merit is rewarded, leaving the mediocre in charge of an unfair system in dire need of reform.

NOTES

1 "Tuition to rise despite funding hike," Alan D. Miller, T*he Columbus Dispatch,* 2 July 1993, p. 1A.
2 Charles W. Anderson, *Prescribing the Life of the Mind* (Madison, Wis.: Univ. of Wisconsin, 1993), p. x.
3 Milton Greenberg, "Accounting for Faculty Members' Time," *The Chronicle of Higher Education,* 20 October 1993, p. A68.
4 "Corporate America's New Lesson Plan," Lori Bongiorno, *Business Week,* 25 October 1993, p. 103.
5 "Securing the Future of Higher Education in Ohio: A Report of the Ohio Board of Regents," December 1992, p. 17.
6 "What It Takes for Professors to Get Themselves Fired," by Jacob Neusner, *The Chronicle of Higher Education,* 17 March 1993, p. 52A.

Four

DUBIOUS REWARDS

[N]o sensible person can have great confidence in what emerges from our evaluation processes. Some such processes are better than others but all are essentially flawed.

GUIDO STEMPEL

PROFESSORIAL DUTIES

In 1988, the U.S. Department of Education described the combined professoriate as containing 489,000 individuals. Men dominated the ranks at 72.7%. Some 89.5% of the men and women in academe were white, and 54% held a doctorate degree. As for rank, 33.1% were full professors, 23.7% associate, 22.8% assistant, 11.5% instructor, and 1.6% lecturer, with the rest having different titles or none.

The profile of the professoriate will change dramatically in the next 20 years. According to some estimates, nearly all professors teaching now in two- and four-year colleges will be replaced.

No such estimates to my knowledge exist concerning department heads, chairs, directors, deans, provosts and presidents, typically because they tend to step down after a relatively brief term and join the professoriate full-time. At some schools, while they still are in office, the salaries of these faculty administrators are averaged with those of regular teachers because the university president, earning, say, $125,000 per year, might lecture occasionally in his or her specialty and hold the rank of professor. (They might be expected to teach one class per semester, but nobody usually checks.) In any case, when these administrators resign and become teachers again, they take their old salaries or part of their old salaries with them, inflating average salaries for full professors.

In their powers and freedoms, these faculty administrators differ greatly from support staff administrators who, essentially, run the university. Support staff handles chores such as admissions, grant writing, funding, surveys, registration, library functions, and the like, and generally have business-like jobs and personalities. They may teach a class part time or on overload, but they lack tenure and so can be fired when they criticize the academy or say something controversial. They tend to be quiet for that reason. They work 55-hour weeks on incomes that also are set across the board by many legislatures, and they receive no overtime. Although their jobs are as hectic and demanding as those in the business world, they receive no bonuses or perks. They do not travel with their spouses to Maui for confabs on motivating union staff. They answer to deans, provosts, or presidents and provide them with data, strategies, solutions and, in tough budgetary times, excuses. However, the one advantage support staff administrators have over professors is a clearly defined job description.

Consider this rather typical one for Associate Director of the Graduate Division at the Wharton School of the University of Pennsylvania: "Duties will include the coordination, management, and oversight of the administration and delivery of academic services for 1,500 students in the MBA program. This position, reporting to the Vice Dean and Director, is high profile and results oriented."

That's tough business talk. The last two words of the description mean: *You can be fired.*

That fact is usually on the mind of a middle manager. He or she works in an environment where others enjoy job security and knows, in tough economic times, support staff is the first to go. One such manager in an academic support unit at a state university describes his job thusly: "I do my work as quickly and correctly as I can, and make everyone else on my staff do the same." When I noted that this sounded like the United Press International motto—"Get it first, get it fast, get it right"—he agreed, adding this phrase: "and keep myself out of trouble."

In many ways, this also is how untenured professors feel. They lack job security but, unlike middle managers, take positions with very broad responsibilities. Business executives would never define jobs the way administrators in academe do, outlining duties above and beyond a potential employee's capabilities. Entry-level business employees may work long and hard hours, but at tasks that they come to know quickly and in depth. Moreover, probationary periods last between six and twelve months, so the non-acceptable employee is cut without too much fanfare or emotional investment. In academe, untenured men and women work furiously for five to seven years before they go up for tenure, a bargain for the taxpayer; however, often they are let go because the university can document that they did not fulfill *all* of their obligations as stated in their contracts. While most industrious untenured professors do receive tenure, even if they do not fulfill all their duties, some don't for trivial reasons during economic downturns, when legislatures cut budgets. Word comes from the top of the Ivory Tower, and these otherwise deserving untenured individuals are fired. Either they sigh in relief and rejoin the business community or take a breath and an untenured professorship elsewhere, bracing for another five to seven years of hazing.

Here is a typical listing reprinted from the "Want Ad" section of a 1993 issue of *The Chronicle of Higher Education:* "The University of Northern Iowa is seeking to fill a tenure-track position within the College of Natural Sciences at the assistant professor level with an appointment in one of the science disciplines (biology, chemistry, earth science, or physics). The appointment will begin in August of 1994. This full-time position includes teaching assignments in Science Education both at the undergraduate and graduate levels; teaching courses in a science discipline, student advisement; science education research and writing; grant procurement; and service to the academic community. Salary is competitive."

It had better be competitive. What scientist in his or her left brain would take a job with such a broad range of duties in the private sector? The upshot is that the unlucky candidate for this post will have to be writing grants during weekends, in essence earning his or her own salary. This emphasis may lower teaching effectiveness. And you can count on a legislator criticizing time spent by this person doing research, without realizing that without such research—which helps fund positions like this one—the education budget would have to be increased to hire more teachers.

Here is another listing in my discipline: "University of the Pacific. Assistant Professor in Print Journalism, tenure track position, for Fall 1994 appointment. Responsibilities: Teach such courses as Beginning and Advanced News Writing, Publications Editing, Introduction to Mass Communication, Mass Media Law and Ethics. Advise student newspaper and supervise students in newspaper practicum or internship experiences. Qualifications: Ph.D. required. Excellence in teaching and scholarly research, and professional experience in journalism are required for appointment, tenure and promotion."

This advertisement says nothing about advising, service, or university and community work, but one can be certain the unlucky applicant will be evaluated on some or all of these missing components.

Take a closer look at the requirements for this position, if you think education is early retirement. I can tell you candidly that advising a student newspaper is a full-time nightmare job. You can get fired over details beyond your control. I almost did at *The Daily O'Collegian* at Oklahoma State when one of my reporters disclosed that the new veterinary medicine building could not be named after one of our politicians, because a little-known law forbade it. Some of the regents, gubernatorial appointees of the same political party, became irate.

However, the University of the Pacific, hiring at the low-paid assistant professor level, wants a newspaper adviser and more: The applicant must have print media experience, a doctoral degree (few working professionals do), teach required courses that demand skill and expertise (lead-writing to law-analysis), and crunch data for articles in scholarly journals. In truth, there are only a handful of people capable of doing this in the entire world, so the assistant professor will not only be working 60-hour weeks but also learning on the job. At the end of five to seven years, perhaps he or she will have learned enough to meet tenure, providing, of course, that the assistant professor has not criticized or alienated colleagues and the governor is not cutting budgets and bashing academe. If so, someone will claim that the fired assistant prof did not fulfill contractual obligations.

Many released professors hang their heads and go. Others sue.

Finally, a listing from the Arts: "The Department of English (at Gettysburg College) invites applications for a two-year position beginning August 1994 at the instructor or assistant professor level for someone qualified to direct a writing center and coordinate a first-year composition program. Besides administrative duties, teaching responsibilities include composition, advanced composition, literary survey(s), and possibly a literature course in the professor's area of specialization. We are particularly interested in a person who can add an alternative perspective to our department in terms of culture, special interests, or theoretical approach."

Again, note the broad range of professional and scholarly skills required for the two-year position. This candidate will administrate a nightmarish program—a freshman writing program. (You can't get fired for doing this poorly as easily as you can advising a student newspaper, but it is very wearing, given the language skills of most undergraduates.) What is particularly bothersome about this ad, however, is that it seems to hold out a carrot—the professor may or may not be allowed to teach a course in his or her own specialty—and, if that is not enough, blatantly makes a pitch for cultural diversity. In essence, the department would be happy to hire a black woman to suffer these duties without tenure in return for the opportunity to share her African-American values. (If diversity is so important in this department, the applicant should be offered a tenure-track post.)

What these three typical ads have in common is The Bargain. The governing boards and/or regents of these three unremarkable schools will be getting three remarkable employees at low cost. The tenured faculties at University of the Pacific and Northern Iowa will work these employees to the bone and then either grant or withhold tenure. At Gettysburg, the nontenure-track culturally diverse person will be worked to the bone, too, and then let go according to her contract. (If she excels and the budget allows, she may be offered a tenure-track position, requiring another few years of hard labor.) At any rate, if these applicants make the cut and get tenure, they may relax for a few semesters, improving their teaching.

Then they get ready for Round Two: promotion.

RESEARCH VERSUS TEACHING

After earning tenure, doing the bulk of the department's work, assistant professors learn the system. Typically they have served on evaluation committees or have had access to annual review data and know the ropes by which they can hang themselves (and others). They will have to do some research if they hope to be promoted.

Research is defined broadly, according to the academic discipline. In a creative writing department, it can be a poem published in a literary magazine. In a humanities department, it can be an essay and in the social sciences, an article in a refereed journal. In the sciences, it can be an experiment or a project underwritten by government or industry. However defined, research is difficult to schedule when a professor can easily spend a 40-hour week teaching, advising, doing service and independent studies, grading, preparing lectures, mentoring student groups, and directing honors tutorials, theses, and dissertations.

This is why many professors who do research also resent it. Yet they conduct it because they want to be promoted after ten or twelve years in academe. Many will quit at this point and become career teachers or bitter associate professors, doomed to retire at that rank. Others with doctoral degrees who meet minimal requirements for research—a study or two each year in my discipline—will eventually attain the title of full professor.

Research is necessary at the university level. Without it, a teacher in a professional or science discipline like journalism or chemistry will have to return to the newsroom or laboratory periodically; otherwise, his or her lectures will be outdated and students will be misinformed. Professors in the arts and humanities will have to create art work or analyze literature and society, publishing their creations or interpretations in the appropriate journals. Otherwise in class they will become mediums of somebody else's epiphanies and their students will learn second-hand truths out of homogenized books. Moreover, as noted earlier, research helps defray costs. When business and government complain about research, they usually forget they rely on it for projects and development. When voters complain about research, they usually forget that professors who do it have friends in the business world and so are able to get jobs for their students—in sum, why parents sent their children to college in the first place—by placing a call or composing a letter to the right person.

Students know this, of course. Ask them whom they usually solicit when requesting recommendations for jobs or graduate schools; they go to the "researchers," not the "teachers." In the past two years, I have been able to place four of my graduates with F&W Publications in Cincinnati because I write a column for one of its magazines. I have been able to send five of my students to one creative writing program because of my reputation as a poet and writer. Students listen to my lectures because they know that I am informed as a researcher. They treat other researchers on my faculty similarly—two of whom have found time to mentor student groups—and in return, they get jobs and fellowships at graduate schools because these teachers have influential friends and colleagues. Students may adore professors who teach but do no research, spending hours in their offices, but as graduation nears, they know that these instructors lack name-recognition and clout.

Students feel much differently about career teachers when it comes to advising and service. They know that the researchers are busy with projects and so ask career teachers to guide them through academic straits or participate in student organizations. These are essential activities that career teachers usually make time for while missing colleagues do research. The problem is not that research is considered more important than teaching but that advising and service, which career teachers have time for, are not weighted heavily in annual reviews.

Nonetheless, education-bashers, the media, and state lawmakers have focused exclusively on the teaching-research debate. When you read their books or reports, you come away feeling that everyone in the university is doing research and nobody is teaching and the few professors who teach are not appreciated or rewarded. In reality, the vast majority of professors do not publish much after they earn tenure. According to a 1989-90 survey conducted by the University of California at Los Angeles Higher Education Research Institute, almost 45.3% of faculty at all institutions didn't have a piece of writing accepted for publication or published in the last two years. Only 25.7% had 1 or 2 items accepted or published, with 15.8% having 3-4 pieces; 10.8%, 5-10 pieces; 1.9%, 11-20 pieces; 0.4%, 21-50 pieces; and 0.1%, 50 or more pieces.

Of course, one professor's scholarly article in a refereed journal may require as much effort as another professor's fifty poems in little magazines. However, these statistics are valuable precisely because they are so inclusive. Furthermore, fully 98.2% of respondents said that teaching was considered "essential" or "very important" as a professional goal while 58.5% said that "research" was. Only 29.2% rated committee work highly and only 43.4% thought service via committee work was essential or very important as a goal. Advising, predictably, wasn't included in the survey. [1]

Given those statistics, however, widely distributed reports like one by Jon Meachem in *The Washington Monthly,* make little sense: "The real issue is why universities have let research become the alpha and omega of their culture. Because good teaching is assumed, the present system of professorial evaluation allows bad teaching to go undetected and unremedied. This means that professors who do well in the public sphere of publication rise to the top, leaving teaching stars in a professional steerage class."[2]

Meachem quotes statistics from the Carnegie Foundation that claim only 58 percent of faculty in four-year schools say their chief interest lies in the classroom. Data for all schools should be used because readers assume that all of academe is reflected in those numbers. As it turns out, the statistic in the California study is 97.6% for professors who claim teaching is "essential" or "very important" as a goal at four-year state universities, Meachem's target. Some 78.6% rank research that highly. The statistics mean, simply, that both activities are important if a professor has set goals to achieve tenure and promotion. But Meachem uses his statistic to imply that teaching no longer is important in academe and that outside interests, like research, are because of prevailing philosophies. A more likely interpretation might be that the Carnegie respondents already know how to teach, so their goals—finally getting a grant written to underwrite research and keep a job, finding time to compose a book chapter, locating a publisher, consulting with business to make ends meet—might indeed reside outside the Ivory Tower.

Meachem states that the average pay for a full professor is $65,000 "for about 90 minutes of class time a day for the eight months a year that school is in session. Not a bad deal at all."

I can think of better deals. Meachem makes it seem that showing up for class is all that professors do. Imagine how misleading such an assertion would sound if applied to a surgeon or a lawyer; the professor has to prepare before entering a classroom, just as a surgeon or lawyer must prepare before entering the operating room or the court room. A professor delivers a speech eight to twelve times per week. I know executives in publishing and advertising who spend the better part of a month preparing to deliver a speech to their respective associations.

Furthermore, I know of no professor working on an eight-month contract, as Meachem indicates. Most are for nine or ten months. And he is using $65,000 without adjusting for years in rank (more on that later). Ironically he quotes my University as a leader in its class according to merit considerations: "At Ohio University in Athens—a 19,000-student school with nearly 16,000 undergraduates—there's a flexible way to figure salaries. If a physics professor, for instance, wants to be judged more on teaching, his annual salary can be computed 60 percent for teaching performance, 20 percent for research, and 20 percent for service instead of the more familiar 40/40/20 formula."

To which I replied, when I first read this, "I wish somebody would have told me that."

This is the trouble with such reports. They skim the surface of academe and misguide the public with surface truths. Indeed, a department at Ohio University may figure merit the way Meachem reports, but not all departments do. Some older full professors with administrative experience may earn $65,000 per year, but many middle-aged full professors do not, and the latter are, in some cases, more productive, in as much as they have earned full professor status earlier in their careers.

Such untruths also influence legislators. In his article "Faculty Bashing: Some Implications for Mass Communication Professors," fellow journalism professor Sam G. Riley at Virginia Polytechnic Institute and State University, takes on several education-reform books that have overinfluenced and misinformed debate. Here is an excerpt of Riley's attack on economist Martin Anderson's *Impostors in the Temple:* "At top universities, [Anderson maintains] full professors average $80,000 in salary. (By neglecting to define 'top universities,' [Anderson] allows readers to assume this figure pertains to most large universities. The actual figure for research universities is something closer to $63,000: full profs in our field [journalism] average far less.)"[3]

Riley calls Anderson's bluff when the economist states most

schools subsidize faculty housing (a "few" do, Riley corrects, not "most"). Riley knows the impact of disinformation. He quotes Anderson—"About the only thing missing is door-to-door limousine service"—and warns: "Just let your state representatives read that line, and see how you fare in the next appropriations cycle."

When the administration of Ohio governor George Voinovich first heard exaggerated published reports about higher education, he organized a task force and conducted hearings. At one such hearing, the Legislative Office of Education Oversight (no pun was intended) released a report stating that research plays a big role in promotion and tenure decisions. Nobody seemed to be asking how much research, exactly, was getting done at our institutions. Although fond of implying that faculty were lazy, lawmakers did not deduce that it might be in the non-productive professor's interest to shirk research obligations and publish nothing for years on end. Nobody made a case for teamwork, either, illustrating how researchers and teachers complement each other and serve students in the ways that I have noted earlier. The Voinovich administration did learn, however, that government, too, played a role in the emphasis on research. Elaine Hairston, chancellor of the Ohio Board of Regents, remarked that the state, "through a research challenge program, is providing funding to stimulate research for needed economic development. And when the state cuts funding to higher education—as it has in the past three years—professors are encouraged to pursue research as a source of money. ... If the state wants a stronger emphasis on teaching," Hairston concluded, "it must have a counterbalance to that stream of income."[4]

Lawmakers rejected a proposal that would have rewarded teaching excellence. When forced to put its money where its mouth was, the Legislature underwrote research and gagged on its own propaganda.

But all this is moot. In an academic socialist system, there are only two statistics that matter with regard to compensation. The most important one is the starting salary. Then it's years in rank.

GOOD AND BAD DEALS

A good teacher attempts to improve himself or herself and motivate students. He or she does research because it lends credibility to lectures and helps students get jobs in industry or fellowships in graduate schools. A bad teacher is generally non-productive as a researcher and abuses tenure and rank, hindering intellectual growth; he or she may even lie, harass, or intimidate students in the classroom.

Those are my distinctions. How do others define the good and bad professor?

Good professors have common traits, according to a study of 31 teachers selected as "outstanding" at Ohio University. These have been elected "University Professors" by the student body. They are put through a rigorous selection process. Students vote for teachers during registration. Votes are adjusted to reflect enrollment, so that the teacher with the most students does not always win. Members of a student committee sit in on classes, interrogate finalists in interviews, and ask to see course outlines. In the Ohio study, *Perceptions of Teaching Excellence* by Milton E. Ploghoft, students said that the "good professor knows the subject matter; is organized and methodical; cares about students; is available for conferences; and encourages students to work hard, to think for themselves, and to listen to and accept other students' opinions. Above all, the good professor is enthusiastic about teaching."[5]

When a teacher wins a University Professor award at Ohio University, or a similar Amoco Foundation award at Oklahoma State and other universities, he or she gets $2000 for books and supplies. Then the money is withdrawn from the salary the next year.

Distinction is fleeting in academe.

In general, administrators treat good and bad members of their faculties similarly when distributing raises. In times of plenty, a good teacher may get a merit award of one or two percentage points over the bad counterpart's raise. (Even this can become political with merit "shared" in a department.) However awarded, the merit raise—a token thirty or forty dollars each month—is tantamount to the price of a reference book or pocket calculator.

The situation is worse at universities whose faculty are represented by unions. Now administrators get to deal with the professoriate across the board *by invitation,* avoiding the issue of individual and departmental excellence. Usually they agree to smaller increments for raises than are awarded by the state but promise to adjust salaries by rank instead of by merit. By doing so they save significant sums and can divert the remainder of their budgets—as much as half, in isolated cases—to administrative support staff that extends from the library to the athletic program. This distribution confuses taxpayers who believe their money is being used for teaching when it is being used for something else.

A similar problem exists at the departmental level. Just as there are good and bad professors at each university, there are good and bad programs. However, many administrators—some at the best institutions—are reluctant to acknowledge that certain departments are superior to others; typically, the amount set aside for the best three departments on campus is about the same as that of the worst three. The impact is felt throughout the institution because it undercuts morale. It homogenizes. Thus, administrators who undercut teamwork and mission in such manner end up promoting mediocrity instead of "excellence," a standard cliché that has more to do with flag-waving than with quality in the classroom.

In truth, there is no substantial way to reward excellence in academe. True, an administrator can take a productive researcher or top teacher out of the laboratory or classroom to chair a program for a few years. Then the professor in question can return to the lab or classroom with a decent salary. As an administrator, the professor will receive incentives in addition to across-the-board raises. At many schools, administrators keep such raises when they step down and teach again.

In academic socialism, as in *Animal Farm* by George Orwell, *all professors are equal, but some are more equal than others.*

It happens at all levels. At one school in 1993, a president with six years of service reportedly resigned at the start of the fall semester and left to teach elsewhere in the state system, retaining her $100,000 salary. Such practices may prompt professors like Sam G. Riley to deduce: "If faculty were really in the driver's seat, would administrators' salaries so far outdistance ours?"[6] In higher education, you can be paid more for doing less if you also are an administrator with a failsafe contract.

That is academe's dirty little secret.

LIFETIME INEQUITIES

Over the course of a 30-year career in academe, productive professors earn their keep only if they administrate a few years. Otherwise they only need to do enough research to get by and be promoted after tenure. Why work an extra 15 hours per week creating or analyzing art and society or crunching numbers and conducting experiments? A 40-hour week will do nicely in an environment lacking substantial rewards and emphasizing accountability. You can arrive at 9 a.m. and take an hour off for lunch and leave for home at 5 p.m., papers graded, students advised, lectures prepared. That leaves you time to mentor a student group one night per week and devote one or two hours to that essay or experiment you hope one day will get done. This usually relates only to men, who outnumber women almost three to one in academe. If you are a woman, you may work 55-hour weeks to appear "average" to some male counterparts who will discount your research or teaching simply because you employ different methods or approaches.

To illustrate, I have designed typical 30-year careers and accompanying salary schedules for a faculty chair, productive professor, and an average male and female professor. The chair, productive and average male professor start as assistant professors without tenure earning $20,000 per year. The woman starts with a salary 23% less than her male counterpart, the standard figure used to illustrate gender inequity in higher education.[7] I have built in an economic downturn that lasts seven years; in other words, these careers happen during 23 years of economic prosperity. The charts below illustrate the inequities of administrative perks, the futility of productivity, and the inhumanity of discrimination.

Career of Productive Professor Who Serves Five Years as Chair

Raise % & Merit Adjustments	Years of Service	Annual Salary
5%	1	$20,000
	2	$21,000
	3	$22,050
	4	$23,153
Tenure	5	$24,311
	6	$25,527
	7	$26,803
	8	$28,143
	9	$29,550
$1000/Promotion	10	$32,028
	11	$33,629
	12	$35,310
	13	$37,076
	14	$38,930
Promotion to Director*	15	$44,877
	16	$48,121
	17	$51,527
	18	$55,103
	19	$58,858
5% Return to Faculty	20	$61,801
3% Economic Downturn	21	$63,655
2% Economic Downturn	22	$64,928
0% Economic Downturn	23	$64,928
0% Economic Downturn	24	$64,928
2% Economic Downturn	25	$66,227
3% Economic Downturn	26	$68,214
3.5% Economic Downturn	27	$70,601
4.5%	28	$73,778
	29	$77,098
	30	$80,567

*NOTE: Salary includes $2,000 raise for promotion plus $2,000 incentive in Year 15, with $1,000 incentives annually as chair. A 5% raise was used on the previous year's salary before the raise and/or incentive was added. Salaries in years 15-19 do not include administrative pay during the summer months.

Career of Productive Professor

Raise % & Merit Adjustments	Years of Service	Annual Salary
5%	1	$20,000
	2	$21,000
	3	$22,050
	4	$23,153
Tenure	5	$24,311
	6	$25,527
	7	$26,803
	8	$28,143
	9	$29,550
$1,000/Promotion	10	$32,028
	11	$33,629
	12	$35,310
	13	$37,076
	14	$38,930
$2,000/Promotion	15	$42,877
	16	$45,021
	17	$47,272
	18	$49,635
	19	$52,117
	20	$54,723
3% Economic Downturn	21	$56,365
2% Economic Downturn	22	$57,492
0% Economic Downturn	23	$57,492
0% Economic Downturrn	24	$57,492
2% Economic Downturn	25	$58,642
3% Economic Downturn	26	$60,401
3.5% Economic Downturn	27	$62,515
4.5%	28	$65,328
	29	$68,268
	30	$71,340

NOTE: The $1,000 raise that accompanied promotion to associate professor in Year 10 and the $2,000 raise that accompanied promotion to full professor in Year 15 were added after the percentage raise was applied to the previous year's salary.

Career of Average Professor (Male)

Raise % & Merit Adjustments	Years of Service	Annual Salary
5%	1	$20,000
	2	$21,000
	3	$22,050
	4	$23,153
Tenure	5	$24,311
4.5%	6	$25,405
	7	$26,548
	8	$27,743
	9	$28,991
	10	$30,296
	11	$31,659
$1,000/Promotion	12	$34,084
4%	13	$35,447
	14	$36,865
	15	$38,340
	16	$39,874
	17	$41,469
	18	$43,128
$2,000/Promotion	19	$46,853
3.5%	20	$48,493
3% Economic Downturn	21	$49,948
2% Economic Downturn	22	$50,947
0% Economic Downturn	23	$50,947
0% Economic Downturn	24	$50,947
2% Economic Downturn	25	$51,966
3% Economic Downturn	26	$53,525
3.5% Economic Downturn	27	$55,398
3.5%	28	$57,337
	29	$59,344
	30	$61,421

NOTE: To reflect "average," I decreased the raise percentage by 0.5 after tenure and two promotions in Year 12 and Year 19, reflecting decreasing productivity after each goal. Accordingly I delayed promotion to distinguish this career from that of the productive professor's, assuming the latter would accomplish more earlier.

Career of Average Professor (Female)

Raise % & Merit Adjutsments	Years of Service	Annual Salary
5%	1	$15,400
	2	$16,170
	3	$16,979
	4	$17,828
Tenure	5	$18,719
4.5%	6	$19,561
	7	$20,441
	8	$21,361
	9	$22,322
	10	$23,327
	11	$24,377
$1,000/Promotion	12	$26,474
4%	13	$27,533
	14	$28,634
	15	$29,779
	16	$30,970
	17	$32,209
	18	$33,497
$2,000/Promotion	19	$36,837
3.5%	20	$38,126
3% Economic Downturn	21	$39,270
2% Economic Downturn	22	$40,055
0% Economic Downturn	23	$40,055
0% Economic Downturn	24	$40,055
2% Economic Downturn	25	$40,856
3% Economic Downturn	26	$42,082
3.5% Economic Downturn	27	$43,555
3.5%	28	$45,079
	29	$46,657
	30	$48,290

A careful analysis shows that for five years' work as chair, with a reduced teaching load, that professor will retire earning almost $10,000 more in Year 30 than his productive counterpart. Over the course of the career, however, the chair will have earned some $108,231 more and that will reflect the standard of living on a fixed income when computed in a pension, resulting in tens of thousands of dollars more, according to individual benefits plans.

The salary difference between the productive and average professor also is about $10,000 upon retirement. The productive professor will have earned $117,001 more than the average counterpart during the span of their careers. However, if one estimates that the productive professor put in a 55-hour week (hardly uncommon) whereas his average counterpart put in a 40-hour week, that would total an extra 480 hours over two semesters each year. If you multiply that by 25 years, excluding years preceding tenure, assuming both worked equally as hard and long, the productive professor put in an extra 12,000 hours. In sum, he was earning $9.75 per hour for each extra hour, about as much as a janitor at Ohio University earns after 120 days of service. The average professor might be less productive, one could argue, but also might have lower stress levels and live longer.

I did not do a productive model for the female professor, because she will probably have to work at that level to *seem* average in a male-dominated work place like academe. I also delayed her promotions for the same reason. Nonetheless, the influence of the starting salary for the average woman speaks for itself in her chart. She is the biggest loser in the academic socialist system. If, in her promotion Year 12, Affirmative Action runs an equity check, she will need about $8,000 to attain parity with her male counterpart. If equity comes in her promotion Year 19, she will need a raise of about $10,000 to attain parity. If either becomes known, as it usually does at state institutions where salaries are public record, and her male counterpart compares this with the $1,000 that accompanied his promotion to associate or the $2,000 that accompanied his promotion to full professor, his morale and the morale of most of the male colleagues will decline in the belief that women get special treatment. Adjustments of this sort only bolster this myth and may be responsible for the "glass ceiling," keeping women from reaching positions of power. But this is subjective. What cannot be denied is the importance of equal pay for equal work *from the start*. Because her starting salary was 77% of her male counterpart, this professor had lost $72,281 over Years 1-12 (if parity happened then) or had lost $134,798 over Years 1-19 (if parity happened then) or had lost $260,991 if parity never occurred over the span of her career.

Upon hearing the influence of academic socialism on women, Alden Waitt, acting director of Women's Studies Program at Ohio University, responded: "I cannot tell you how often I have listened to the problems of women faculty, particularly junior faculty, who outline the overt and insidiously indirect methods used to prevent their advancement in academe. Although I don't think there is some grand conspiracy on the part of men in power (read: usually tall, white, conservative...), I do believe that some men come across as *willfully* ignorant of the old boys' network in which they operate and which they perpetuate. ...."

She continued, "I believe that women academics are frustrated by men in power who devalue them simply because they are women, because they choose to study in or teach in an area such as women's studies, or because they bring with them to the work force actual (horror!) manifestations of 'difference.'

"This last refers to anything that marks the experiences of one sex as different from another, in this case women from men. It can mean childbearing and childrearing responsibilities that the women take on, or it can mean their being penalized for focusing on gender issues by not having those publications or presentations taken into consideration when the women come up for tenure. Or it can mean, simply, that they are hired 'cheaper' because they are women."

Salary inequities are relatively easy to document, Marilyn Greenwald, managing editor of *Newspaper Research Journal* and a colleague of mine in the Journalism School, states. "But I also think there are more subtle inequities, particularly regarding workload and the types of work male and female members are expected to do."

Greenwald notes that, like many female professors, she finds much of her time devoted to service. "Deans, directors and others in power feel they must have a woman on every committee. First, they feel they have the right to advertise that they have women on the faculty. Second, they believe the female minority should be represented on committees.

"It is also women who are by reputation the nurturers. So we are often the ones who are selected to advise student groups. All this means is that while our male colleagues are concentrating on teaching and research (activities that will get them promoted)," Greenwald adds, "we are serving on committees and attending public events that will show our university has hired women.

"So the push to get us hired is also, in a subtle way, keeping us down. I certainly don't believe that this is any kind of conspiracy on the part of university forces. It's a paradox that the same university officials who encourage the hiring of women are also responsible for giving them duties that makes it hard for them to advance."

This paradox that Greenwald mentions often results in "productive" female professors appearing "average" to male counterparts who compare research and teaching achievements, discounting the importance of service. Greenwald recommends that administrators reconsider the effects of service on the careers of female professors. "And we must ask ourselves: is it necessary that all university committees and service activities be composed of men, women, persons of color, etc.? Anyone who can do simple math knows that this puts an undue burden on women and minorities in an institution composed primarily of white males."

Finally, she suggests that it may be the responsibility of women in academe "to just say no—refuse some assignments after service assignments become overburdening."

This is, as indicated earlier, the tenured male response that contributes to volunteerism in the meritless academy.

To gain a broader perspective, I asked a distinguished colleague of mine, Guido Stempel, to discuss the problem of merit in academe. Stempel is the chair of an annual review committee, a nationally known researcher, former editor of *Journalism Quarterly* and now a columnist for *Presstime*, a trade magazine. He responded with the following analysis:

"If you look at salaries for any institution, it may behard to find much evidence of merit. Two years ago one of our faculty members put a complaint in writing with a list of our salaries. I took that list, made assumptions about minimum in rank and the size of annual increments and on the second pass came up with a 'salary schedule' that fit almost perfectly. What that meant was that the only real merit factor was rank. Once in rank your salary was essentially a function of years in rank. Why was that? Well, first of all, the university made an adjustment of associate professor and full professor salaries a few years ago that revolved largely around years in rank. However, I believe, that merely accentuated slightly a trend that was already there. How did it get there?

"There are two ways. The first is small raise pools. You have 4% inflation and a 4% raise pool. The tendency is to make a 3% raise across the board and reserve 1% for merit. If you have, let's say, 10 faculty—3 high merit, 4 merit and 3 no merit, what do you do? First, you give 3% to the no merit people. Then you give 1% to the merit people. That leaves 6% to be divided among the high merit people, or 2% each. So the high merit people get 5%, the merit people get 4% and the no merit people get 3%. That doesn't build a merit-based salary pattern. If the raise pool were 5%, then you could give 3% across the board, add 2% for the merit people and 4% for the high merit people. Then your range would be 3% to 7%. Here at Ohio University, the administration has tended to be cautious about raise pools and has tended to make them smaller than they could have been. That in turn has created little opportunity to reward merit.

"Our situation is not unusual. I said above that the only real merit factor is rank. When you get promoted you usually get something extra. That stays in your salary. If our promotions are based on merit, then rank is a significant merit factor. In the case of the School of Journalism, the problem is compounded by the fact that we have a number of people, I think, of high merit and relatively few of no merit. Our biggest single problem, I think, is that when the raise pool for the university as a whole is 4%, there is no way, despite the demonstrated excellence of our program, that we can get even 5%, much less the 6% that I think we would be entitled to.

"The second problem is how we evaluate. Our teaching evaluations are, in my estimation, essentially invalid. We do them in part so that if we decide someone is not a good enough teacher to get tenure and if he or she sues us, we have something to stand on in court. Yet how would you like to defend our process, even the way the dean wants it done?

Imagine the plaintiff's attorney's questions. Do you know that the people who fill out the form actually are in the class? Are the envelopes kept where they cannot be tampered with? Are the questions valid measures of teaching? Would you say your process evaluates the course of the teacher? Do the answers to the questions really tell you how much the student has learned? Furthermore, if we were really serious about this, we would survey alumni. We did it once, with very different results from what we get in class evaluations.

"On publication, we do a little better, but not much. We attach great importance to publication in refereed journals. Is everything in *Journalism Quarterly* better than everything in *Columbia Journalism Review?* Hardly. I could go on, but the point is that no sensible person can have great confidence in what emerges from our evaluation processes. Some such processes are better than others but all are essentially flawed. In general, the evaluation effort is minimal and superficial. An administrator ought not go overboard in using them as a basis for determining raises. At the same time, one wonders if an administrator shouldn't seek more and better information.

"A lesser factor is that some raises are the result of negotiations by an individual faculty member who feels his or her salary is not high enough. That may take money away from what is in effect the merit pool. At the very least, if there is a merit process functioning, this disturbs it. ...It is also a problem that we have a zero sum game. What we give to A we must take away from Z within the department. What you can give B is in part determined by what you have already given A. No salary decision stands alone.

"Another thought: We have some givens in the system that complicate things. One is that deans should be paid more than faculty members—that the dean should be the highest paid person in the college. Why? Is the manager the highest paid person on the baseball team? Does our dean or any other dean on this campus really contribute more to the good of the institution than you or I do? Does anyone care how much an individual contributes to the good of the institution?"

As Stempel indicates, rewarding merit costs money. Some professors improve teaching or research by spending out of their paychecks for books, travel, and supplies, not to mention longer hours and more responsibility. When education is controlled across the board, such teachers dig deeper into their pockets. They cannot afford to be less effective in the classroom and believe that education is an ideal as important as the self. In essence, there is little in the academic socialist system to reward a professor of true merit. If Professor A wins a Pulitzer Prize for a book and Professor B publishes nothing, if Professor A receives the highest evaluations in the year in which she wins the Pulitzer Prize and Professor B the lowest, and if Professor A does service and exemplary advising and Professor B does none, then Professor A will earn a 7% merit raise and Professor B a 3% one. Depending on the base salary, $40,000 per year say, this represents a token $1,600 extra in Professor A's salary next year. If she does all of the above during an economic downturn, she gets nothing.

Faced with such treatment, good professors move to greener campuses or leave academia.

MERIT SEARCHES

Excellent professors in mid-career often find that by switching jobs they can earn as much as $20,000 more at another university. Sometimes these professors learn, much to their surprise, that they can earn an extra $40,000 by joining government or industry. When a professor tells this to administrators, some challenge the professor to get an offer in writing from another institution, wasting that college's budget and/or taxpayers' money or, in the case of business, corporate funds. The professor brings the offer to the dean, hoping a salary adjustment will be made, reluctant to uproot the family and start over again in another school. If the offer comes from the private sector, the professor will have to give up teaching, his or her passion. If the professor has children or familial responsibilities that require higher salaries, he or she leaves for another institution or abandons the academy.

Bad professors stay put.

When excellent teachers are offered jobs elsewhere, usually administrators do little to keep them. If they did, remaining colleagues would probably complain because the raise pool would be pilfered that year. This is why peer review committees formed to evaluate professor inequity complaints often side against the professor because members know that what they give to a deserving colleague likely will come out of their pockets, not the dean's.

But we commiserate with each other. One night over dinner at my house, Josep Rota, an internationally known communications scholar, calculated how much academic units lose when productive professors leave to take jobs at other universities. Here is his estimate:

Advertising the vacancy	$500
Faculty meetings to define profile of job candidate	$1000
Committee screening of applications	$2000
Candidate evaluation (clerical expenses, travel, room & board)	$5000
Faculty interviews with candidates	$1000
Retraining employee (computer systems, advising, new courses)	$5000
Moving expenses	$2500
Start-up costs (health, payroll, processing, etc.)	$1000
Total Price:	*$18,500*

Rota observed, "Businesses don't allow good employees to leave. But universities do. Given a choice of letting a productive person go or hiring a new one, evaluation committees would always let the excellent one go. This way, money doesn't come out of the raise pool."

Turnover is slow in academe, even in states with legislatures that have frozen salaries and cut higher education budgets, but there comes a point. When a high-profile professor leaves, a replacement is usually made at the assistant professor rank. Often this decision is made at the dean's level to save money, and the difference in salaries is added to the general operating budget. If salaries remain low or fixed and lawmakers keep cutting the budget, soon other productive professors depart. Each time one does, the culture of a department changes accordingly; average or bad professors tend to control the unit because of seniority. Eventually the unit contains a greater number of bad professors who misguide the inexperienced replacements or set impossible or slack priorities.

Then life gets tough for administrators who practice academic socialism. Often they resign at this point and return to the classroom, dipping into the money they managed to save by replacing senior professors with assistants; another search must be done to replace the administrator. If no such money exists, average professors are named as acting directors and the culture changes again.

Now the administrators come under scrutiny by superiors. They have to account for the decline in research and publications, explain why reports are stalled in committee or returned half-baked, and defend questionable tenure and promotion decisions. Lawsuits may get filed. Student complaints may cause more paperwork, and accreditation may be delayed or denied. When this shows up in the five-year plan, a case is made to rehire good professors and pay dearly now to do so. Luring quality teachers is an expensive undertaking for universities that let good teachers go in the past.

The lesson, however, is obvious. No one in academe or state government thinks they should reward merit until an institution's reputation is at stake. In a word, the way to get administrators and legislators to pump money into higher education is not to excel because, they will tell you, no money exists in the budget to reward achievement.

It does exist to circumvent failure.

NOTES

1 Results taken from survey "Attitudes and Activities of Full-Time Faculty Members," 1989-90, appearing in *The Chronicle of Higher Education Almanac*, 25 August 1993, p. 35.
2 "In 'publish or perish' culture, the biggest losers are college students," by Jon Meachem, AlterNet/*The Washington Monthly,* reprinted in *The Athens News*, 18 November 1993, pp. 1, 11-12. Copyright by *The Washington Monthly Company.*
3 "Faculty Bashing: Some Implications for Mass Communication Professors," by Sam G. Riley, *Journalism Educator,* Autumn 1993, p. 72.
4 "Report: Colleges steer professors toward research," by Alan D. Miller, *The Columbus Dispatch,* 14 July 1993, p. 3C.
5 Ploghoft, Milton E. *Perceptions of Teaching Excellence at Ohio University* (Athens, Ohio: Center for Higher Education, 1990), p. 5.
6 Riley, 68.
7 "Trouble at the Top," by Amy Saltzman, *U.S. News and World Report,* 17 June 1991, p. 41.

Five

MERIT MODELS

We have a dictatorship here. If you're lucky, you work your way up the chain to be the chief dictator. ... [T]hat isn't the way it works any more.
Ohio Governor GEORGE VOINOVICH, promoting Total Quality Management

TOTAL QUALITY MANAGEMENT

By the fall of 1993, education-bashing governor George V. Voinovich had encountered total quality management. Like wildfire it is spreading now across the dried-up greens of academe and the brittle branches of government. As soon as the budget situation in Ohio had improved in 1993, Voinovich allocated $580,000 for a new arm of state government called The Office of Quality. (The original program was titled Total Quality Management, but later was changed to "Quality Services Through Partnership" to ease the Orwellian fears of state labor.) Now each of 28 agencies has a TQM specialist, which might prove to be both an investment in Ohio's future and yet another embarrassment to Voinovich. You see, according to TQM's tenets, only about 15% of a company's problems are a direct result of individual employees. The remainder has to do with the system. "The manager's job," writes Ted Marchese in his essay "TQM: A Time for Ideas" in *Change*, is "to drive out blaming and fear, to remove obstacles in the system that prevent persons or teams from doing their best work."[1]

One of the biggest obstacles in higher education in the early 1990s was the governor himself. His platform of accusation had instilled fear, demoralized professors, and lowered productivity. All this was predictable under TQM, and Voinovich—our prophet of accountability—would have been held liable if he operated in the business world instead of the governmental one.

Nonetheless, more than a few professors breathed in relief upon learning that Voinovich was espousing TQM. It might mean that he would praise education periodically and remember the importance of merit and morale. The TQM business philosophy values employees and serves customers, listens to both to solve problems within the system and, as its name indicates, emphasizes quality—from factory floor to board room.

George Keller, chair of the higher education program at the Graduate School of Education of the University of Pennsylvania, believes that TQM probably started on May 16, 1924, "when Walter Shewhart of Bell Labs handed his boss a one-page memo on how the telephone company could use statistical controls to ensure quality in telephone manufacturing."[2] However, its roots may have been earlier, in 1881, when a foreman named Frederick Winslow Taylor in a steel plant studied the concept of "work" and developed ways to enhance it. As Peter F. Drucker writes in *The Wilson Quarterly,* Taylor's "main concern was the creation of a society in which owners and workers, capitalists and proletarians, had a common interest in productivity and could build a relationship of harmony. ..."[3]

One of TQM's founding luminaries was the late W. Edward Deming, a statistical consultant who helped Japanese manufacturers change the image of their products. In the 1950s, "Made in Japan" symbolized "junk"; by the 1980s, the label symbolized "quality." Meanwhile "Made in America" was devalued with the dollar. The impact was felt during the Reagan administration, particularly in the auto industry.

For decades, U.S. car manufacturers had controlled their share of the market. American industrialists like Henry Ford had invented the market. Detroit, however, had forgotten the basics, designing vehicles that looked sharp but that rolled off assembly lines with flaws and broke down after five years—"junk" in the truest sense of the word. The Big Three car companies operated much like state government; they had dictators and bureaucracies. Each department in the upper levels did its own thing and passed its own thing to the next level which in turn passed to the next level and on, finally, to the consumer who footed the bill. The Japanese, meanwhile, were working in teams from the top down and emphasizing quality and service. Consequently, the TQM model has become as much a symbol of auto making as the Model T. Even professors who resist it drive home in Toyotas with Japanese cellular phones.

The Journalism faculty at Ohio University encountered TQM by accident in 1989 during a special faculty meeting. Our school was being considered for a state excellence award, and each one of us had a minute to explain how we contributed to our discipline or students. During that session, we had a glimpse of how our friends and adversaries were sharing individual talents to enhance the program under the directorship of Ralph Izard. One professor with expertise in international journalism spoke about foreign internships that she helped to arrange and coordinate. A computer specialist spoke about how he kept labs up-to-date and emphasized undergraduate advising. The graduate coordinator spoke about the number of papers that master's and doctoral students had presented at a national journalism convention. Another professor mentioned a language test that she developed to improve the grammar and punctuation skills of students. I spoke about the Ohio Magazine Writing Group, the first nonprofit student-run literary agency in a journalism school. At the end of the presentation, I glanced at my colleagues. The faculty was as impressed as the judges, and we won the award.

TQM has its place as a merit model in academe, but right now it fits like a round peg into an oval hole. The peg represents the clearly defined goals and parameters of business; the hole, the broadly defined roles and objectives of academe. For the peg to fit into that hole, university administrators will have to improvise on TQM's tenets if they hope to introduce them to their faculties; otherwise, governors and their political appointees are apt to do so for them, bashing the round pegs into oval holes and fracturing the board structure of academe.

Indeed, it is a time for ideas concerning TQM in education. Ted Marchese's article in *Change* describes the challenges of adapting this business concept so that it enhances higher education. In this section, I'll name four of the six TQM ideas that Marchese thinks are important.[4] I'll make my own adaptations and observations and then consider the ramifications. Finally, I'll move beyond TQM to other merit models in business that may raise morale and reward merit without subverting traditional educational values.

Here are those important TQM tenets:

—*Customer focus*. "The new dispensation is that quality is what the *customer* says it is," Marchese writes. He identifies academic "customers" as everyone linked to the institution, from business advisory boards to undergraduates.

Most professors would agree that the easy route is to let industry dictate curriculum. When that occurs, a university provides little more than vocational-technical training. This means, for instance, that a journalism school may overemphasize technology and underplay philosophy. Typically, when business people serve on advisory boards, they ask administrators to implement programs that solve their short-term rather than long-term needs. Consequently, communication leaders might demand that professors devote more time in their laboratories to desk-top publishing and cable technology than to print history or broadcast ethics. It is no coincidence that most labs in academe are named after business donors and most classrooms after educators.

The news media makes such requests because it lacks the time to train entry-level reporters. However, in addition to professional training built into the curriculum, journalism students are expected to learn everyday skills by working for the campus newspaper or station or by participating in student groups like the Society of Professional Journalists or Advertising Club. They also take summer internships with media outlets or public relations firms.

Media executives know about TQM. They understand its chief dictum when it comes to coverage or programming: *quality is what the customer says it is.* However, they may not understand higher education's traditional goal of developing the mind. The same may be said for executives who hire graduates from the various technical, business, and computer science sequences. True, academe may provide a service by training students for these entry-level jobs. But graduates must be able to synthesize and think; otherwise they may not be able to keep their jobs or advance later in their careers to the executive ranks.

Publishers in particular need to remember this, especially ones who advocate the "nuts and bolts" of journalism and end up with the slings and arrows of libel suits. Business executives generally fire graduates who make mistakes that lead to recalls or litigation. Economists also lose their jobs when they err. So do advertisers, architects, chemists, engineers, stock brokers, bankers, and political and computer scientists.

The challenge then for universities is to provide quality education on two levels—the professional and the intellectual— and balance those seemingly opposite pursuits in curricula, programs and, most importantly, tenure and promotion documents. Advisory board members usually support such a balance, providing that administrators and faculty take time to explain the merits. Imbalances and abuses occur when administrators simply heed business requests without opening dialogues or enlisting the help of professors. Some schools do, including Ohio University. Our director Ralph Izard schedules regular faculty presentations to the board and in turn invites board members to classes, practicing yet another TQM tenet: communication.

Striking a balance between the professional and intellectual also is in the best interests of our chief customer: the student. Typically, undergraduates have two goals. The majority want to find jobs. Administrators may schedule professional courses for that but seldom, if ever, reward professors who procure jobs for graduates. (That's why professors could serve students better in this regard.) Other undergraduates apply for admittance into law, medicine, and graduate programs. They need more traditional course work. But again, professors are not rewarded when they help students prepare for graduate work. Typically, teachers write letters of recommendation. Only a meritorious few make telephone calls to graduate directors of select schools to speak about the research or teaching capabilities of their advisees or to tutor those advisees so that they can pass entry exams like the GRE or LSAT.

In business, employees who focus on the primary needs of customers are rewarded for their efforts. In higher education, they should be too. It is relatively easy to change tenure and promotion documents to reward efforts that lead to jobs or assistantships for students. These efforts also can be documented and measured with letters from advisees in the work force or graduate schools. As indicated earlier, this alone will go a long way in defusing the research-teaching debate in academe. Those who teach well or do pioneering research will have contacts in industry and universities. Those who don't will have to increase their productivity until they procure such contacts. In sum, adapting one tenet of TQM to education often leads to other improvements in the system.

—*Continuous improvement.* Marchese relates this to education: "Somehow, despite all the good will, talent, and effort of individual faculty, there's seldom a collective sense of obligation toward or avidness about the improvement of student learning. So it is that an organization full of learners doesn't add up to a learning organization." To help solve this problem, Marchese notes that once a difficulty that affects learning is detected in an academic unit, it should be dealt with swiftly.

Administrators seldom do this when problems involve professors who intimidate colleagues and abuse tenure. Keep in mind that intimidators often are in their offices. The intimidated go home (and, consequently, abuse tenure because they miss office hours or classes). Professors who caused the morale problem in the first place exploit these abuses, demoralizing their adversaries one more time.

If the cycle continues, cliques evolve and the feuds spread to classrooms, involving and sometimes afflicting students.

Under TQM, neither the intimidator or tenure abuser is to blame as much as the administrator who allowed the infractions to develop. However, if the administrator can detect and solve such problems swiftly, professors know their limits. Intimidators cannot gossip or harass or otherwise subvert and demoralize colleagues because that undercuts teamwork, mission, and morale.

Tenure abusers learn that they have obligations beyond their emotional and professional needs.

Too often, however, administrators ignore these all-too-common scenarios. There is little they can do to stop feuds, they claim, because professors in question have earned tenure. (This is why business people and legislators target tenure repeatedly in academic-reform proposals when actually the focus should be on administrators.) When administrators embrace this excuse, they shirk their duties, waste taxpayer money they are paid extra to handle such problems, contribute to the feud by allowing it to continue, undercut plans, worsen morale, and imperil academic freedom.

Again, the system of built-in rewards is to blame. Department heads, chairs, and directors (not to mention deans) should receive incentives when they deal with and solve personnel problems that affect undergraduate instruction. They can put an end to needless arguments by taking action on curricula matters, for example, instead of allowing the usual factions to battle it out and waste time in meetings. They can encourage research in an area of specialization that the unit lacks—prosody in poetry, say, or chaos in physics. They can bust cliques via committee assignments or discourage gossip or outright name-calling by keeping detailed notes and confronting abusers.

Administrators can do something about personnel problems. Tenure is no obstacle. Not long ago administrators used tenure as an excuse to sidestep cases involving sexual harassment or racial discrimination. That has changed, largely because of peer and social pressure. Administrators may still not be able to detenure sexual harassers or racists, but they certainly do deal with them or are themselves held accountable.

Similarly, administrators have powers that can end arguments and temper other abuses. First, they can listen. Often the motives of trouble-makers or tenure-abuses reveal weaknesses in the basic management. Administrators also have power to change the system and ease the unspoken fears and/or highlight the contributions of the parties in question. If both sides refuse to change their behavior, administrators can say "No." No to travel requests. No to conventions. No to speakers. No to a dozen other academic privileges that troublesome professors take for granted. And when they storm into the administrator's office, as they invariably will do, he or she can offer to say "Yes" ... in return for a change in behavior or attitude. When the change occurs, the administrator can write a note of thanks or appreciation and file a copy with the dean, documenting efforts to solve problems on a continual basis.

For that, the administrator deserves a reward.

—*People.* Marchese writes: "An organization avid for improvement sees people as its greatest resource. It does everything possible to give an employee the preparation, tools, and initiative to contribute to corporate goals." Of course, an academic unit has to have some goals in the first place if they are to be improved upon and if people are to be rewarded.

Goals will vary according to academic units. A common one, however, is to view the teaching specialties or research interests of individual professors as pieces of a mosaic that, when combined, constitute a vision. This not only emphasizes teamwork and shared mission but also increases morale—without increasing the budget.

Every professor *should* have an identity within the mosaic of an academic unit. In our English department at Ohio University, for instance, you can tell visitors who admire the writing of John Milton to see Roy Flannagan, editor of the *Milton Quarterly*. In our Journalism School, you can tell visitors who are concerned about correct language use in media reports to see Drusilla Evarts. The problem is that some professors in the English department or Journalism School, for that matter, have no such identities. Because of specialization in the sciences, this problem seems to happen more in the arts and humanities. Typically, you might find four poets in the creative writing department. In such a case, an administrator needs to promote the outside or research interests of these individuals. One poet may be particularly knowledgeable in literatures from other countries. Another may be an effective workshop leader and another, a skilled adviser. Yet another might know about publishing because he or she edits a literary magazine.

In sum, an administrator has to ensure that each person in his or her unit, including staff workers, has such an identity; employees who do, even if underpaid or mistreated, have clearly defined roles and personal goals that may keep them productive.

Too many administrators hesitate to make such distinctions. What would happen, they worry, if Professor A is identified as a media critic when Professor B and C also write media criticism? Conflicts or arguments might occur, and then what will we do? Consequently, the academic socialist says that everyone critiques media equally as well. The real question may be: Why does a journalism school need three media critics when it teaches only one media criticism class twice a year? Again, in solving a morale problem, one might find weaknesses in the system concerning hiring practices or lack of goals, missions, or visions at the administrative level. In such a case, the administrator responsible for this may need some retraining in basic management skills.

Marchese writes: "In companies like Motorola, Corning, or GM's Saturn Division, a remarkable 5 percent of the company's expenditures are devoted to employee education, training, and development." Another article in Business Week states that business spends $15 billion a year on training and education of employees and managers.[5] Marchese asks: "Why is it that in almost any university or college—organizations devoted to learning—the comparable expenditure will be a fraction of one percent?"

Answer: Administrators are not accountable.

—*Benchmarking*. Simply, this jargon-word means the ability to identify and share effective practices. Marchese briefly cites innovations in student advisement, the teaching of writing, and the deployment of technology in academe. "[T]he observable fact is that most of these innovations have gone nowhere," he laments.

Again, Marchese is on point. Professors should share their teaching successes, research-related discoveries or publishers and agents with colleagues, especially untenured ones. Too many fear that by helping a colleague, they will be shortchanging themselves. First of all, as documented earlier, any shortchanging amounts to pocket change when merit raises are doled out in academe. But two other problems hinder benchmarking in higher education. Many professors lack specific identities and so are reluctant to share successes that help define themselves or outside interests. More importantly, however, the system does not reward professors who help other professors in the spirit of teamwork and mission.

Such contributions also are easy to document. In the past year I helped two colleagues at my university and more than a dozen outside my institution prepare book proposals for publishers. Routinely I provide the names of editors and agents and even make introductions when appropriate for other professors. When I keynoted the National Association of Newspaper Columnists at its annual meeting in Columbus a few years ago, I gave the organizer the name and phone number of a colleague in the magazine sequence.

When she published a textbook on magazine editing with

Longman, I tacked a copy of the cover on the bulletin board next to my office door so my advisees would see it. Moreover, I do not expect similar treatment from my colleague. I show her such courtesies because I admire what she does. Some professors and students consider us rivals; I don't.

And that makes all the difference.

This is part of the vision that TQM offers with its emphasis on merit, morale, people, service, efficiency, teamwork, improvement and quality.

Here is a skeptic's description of the TQM vision in academe, composed by George Keller, who questions its applicability to higher education: "[S]tudents are treated courteously by everyone—from security to registrars—from the moment they first walk into the admissions office till they die as alumni; where professors teach with motivational brilliance and advise students frequently and wisely; where maintenance personnel fix leaky faucets and replace burnt-out light bulbs almost immediately and clerks deliver campus mail swiftly and with a smile; where reimbursement checks for faculty travel expenses arrive the next day; and where the campus has buildings, shrubbery, and quiet, beautiful groves designed to help students contemplate, discuss serious issues and write poetry."[6]

You may note that the administrator is missing in Keller's mosaic.

Nonetheless his vision, as Keller openly acknowledges, is a long way off. He correctly notes that students are a "product" of their families, backgrounds, and communities as well as creatures of their own self-discipline, ambitions, and wills. "If anything," he states, "U.S. Education may already cater too much to 'customer satisfaction' and may need a heavy dose of more demanding teaching and rigorous, directed study to prepare (students) for the fierce competition in world markets rather than teaching and services to please the students as if they were purchasers of hi-fi equipment."[7]

But Keller has his hopes, too. He is chair of the higher education program at the Graduate School of Education of the University of Pennsylvania and seems concerned that traditional educational values will be undermined by the rush to introduce and apply TQM tenets to academe. I agree. We should adapt and implement appropriate merit models and then gauge their short-term and long-term effectiveness. But

I also would much rather take my models from business than from government or allow the latter to institute business models by mere decree.

That's why I'm writing this book.

MERIT MARGINS

Richard Chait, professor of higher education and management at the University of Maryland at College Park, is a critic of visions—especially at the presidential levels. According to Chait, "Presidential visions influence faculty work life about as much as political party platforms shape the day-to-day decisions of governmental agencies."[8] Instead he would eliminate that part of TQM and use its tenets to improve the basics—especially, again, at the presidential level: "Without vision," he writes, "presidents should also have ample time to discover and facilitate the most attractive and feasible aspirations of academic and administrative units. Who knows, time may even be available for presidents to perform small and vastly underestimated acts of leadership such as returning phone calls promptly, responding to memoranda, arriving punctually for meetings, listening intently to the concerns of others, and following up swiftly. In other words, presidents might adhere to a basic and sensible tenet of TQM: Do the ordinary extraordinarily well."

To some, even this modest vision may seem a long way off.

In truth, the round peg of TQM is better suited to the round peg of academic support systems that are business-oriented anyway. Even Keller notes that at the University of Pennsylvania a vice president who employed TQM tenets saved millions on trash removal, billable charges, and reduced paperwork; moreover, he adds, other universities cut down transcript requests from 90 days to five.

At the University of Denver, administrators have instituted another concept loosely associated with TQM: gain-sharing. After continually losing money and selling off millions of dollars of property to pay bills, trustees recruited Daniel L. Ritchie, a semi-retired executive of the Westinghouse Broadcasting Company, to serve as chancellor. Ritchie turned the university around so that it now boasts annual surpluses.

Administrators at Denver welcome comparisons of education with business.

James. R. Griesemer, treasurer and vice-chancellor for business and financial affairs at Denver, states: "It's both artificial and dysfunctional to talk about the 'business' side of the university as distinct from the 'academic' side. It's as artificial as drawing a distinction between teaching and research. You can't have one without the other."[9]

Essentially Griesemer is correct. Not only is education still perceived as an offshoot of the 19th-century "factory" model, recruiting raw material at registration and turning out finished products at graduation, it is a partner with business almost at every school and college. Donors, regents, and alumni represent the business world. Corporate executives spend weeks on end at campuses across the country, learning new business methods or brushing up on basics. In fact, some 5,170 executives attended classes and/or campus seminars in 1992 while management professors at McGill, Columbia, Virginia and Michigan, to name a few schools, worked with executives on a regular basis.[10] For a more complete picture, add to this figure the thousands of professors who consult with business, sharing their knowledge or research, especially in the social and hard sciences.

At the University of Denver, a private school, administrators and faculty are expected to recruit to maintain enrollments. When they do, they are rewarded according to adapted principles of gain-sharing—a management concept that became popular in the early 1980s when the University of Denver was losing money as an institution.

Before evaluating how gain-sharing might work in academe, let's see how it works in business. Two decades ago, advances in technology were forcing many U.S. companies to retool or relocate or risk losing profits to competitors who could afford the latest innovations. This was the situation with one Ed Rogan, owner of a plastic-knob manufacturing company, profiled by Tom Ehrenfeld in the trade magazine *Inc*. Rogan's employees did not care about his plight; much like professors, they anticipated annual raises whether or not he made a profit. Rogan considered and rejected moving his operation from Illinois to Mexico and finally hit on gain-sharing. In sum, the strategy would peg worker productivity to profits. Simply, Rogan and his executives set goals and workers became more efficient to meet them and enjoy any surpluses[11]. According to Ehrenfeld, employees at Rogan were satisfied with the new emphasis on merit, receiving what amounted to 16.3% raises in the first 18 months.

The problem with gain-sharing, as every chief executive knows, is that goals must be realistic so that they can be met. Otherwise employees resent the effort to make them work harder in a rigged system that offers no rewards. As Ehrenfeld puts it: "For a gain-sharing plan to succeed, employees must see the link between their performance and pay."[12]

Faculty and administrators at the University of Denver call gain-sharing "shared responsibility." The setup rewards employees who cut spending, recruit, and raise funds. Money saved is shared with the academic unit and university. Departments keep half of what they earn and can spend a third of that without the approval of administrators (although they cannot hire permanent staff members).

There are potential problems with this model. The emphasis on savings can lead to lower starting salaries, especially for women. The shared responsibility motif and the focus on outside business concerns, like recruiting and fund-raising, can undermine the identity crisis that afflicts academe. Too many professors will be known by the number of students recruited or the amount of dollars raised, rather than by their research or specialties; consequently, competition can undermine such TQM concepts as benchmarking, where professors help each other for the common good. Another drawback with gain-sharing occurs during unforeseen shortfalls or financial mismanagement—a losing portfolio, for example—that cannot be offset by recruiting, fund-raising, cost-cutting, hard-working professors. Finally, the gain-sharing model broadens the already too-broad job descriptions typical professors.

Nonetheless, the benefits at the University of Denver are obvious, too. For one, professors are still employed. Moreover, the emphasis on teamwork, goals, and rewards is a morale-booster. The greater lesson here is obvious, as well: Universities willing to adapt merit models from business can indeed incorporate them into their structures—if motivated to do so—while still maintaining traditional educational values, as Denver does.

BEYOND TQM

Certainly, education should take the best of what business has to offer. Administrators should adapt those merit models to maintain educational values. No one, least of all me—a professor of ethics—would promote the worst that business has to offer; unethical scandals abound, from pyramid schemes to ad campaigns targeting the unemployed or disenfranchised. Neither do universities raid each other the way corporations do (minority hiring notwithstanding), engineer take-overs, and bilk stockholders of life-savings. True, some faculty administrators may retain their salaries when they step down, but benefit packages for corporate executives can be downright obscene. Confronted with evidence, some business types argue that their executive pay agreements do not come out of taxes, as they do in academe; they are right. They come out of what is left after citizens pay their taxes, equally immoral. For obvious reasons, neither do educators want to follow business' lead when it comes to social issues like equality or diversity. There are relatively few female and minority top executives at Fortune 500 companies. As for starting salaries for women, female financial managers earn 67% of their male counterparts' salaries; female personnel and labor relations employees earn 69%, and women sales people earn a lowly 58%, all below the 77% of what female professors earn in higher education.[13]

To discover merit models beyond TQM, educators should look to small and midsize businesses run by women. Many such companies used to be called "Father and Son" or "Mom and Pop" concerns. Now they are apt to be "Mother and Daughter" or "Daughter and Daughter" or "Mom and Mom." Discouraged by the lack of equality and diversity in big business, along with limits of the glass ceiling, many women have pioneered companies that set new standards with regard to merit and morale. Regardless of the gender of owners, the key to their successes often is a strong foundation of values—sometimes spiritual values—ones that academe has abandoned.

Professors snickering now upon reading that sentence should re-evaluate their lives. Typically, they seek security so that they can study and practice specialties in the arts and humanities. Many do not know how a person in business feels when he or she has to put everything on the line—their bank accounts and retirement funds, their children's college money, a second mortgage and loans—to open a business, hire people, and be responsible for their welfare and families, too.

Such risk often inspires prayer.

Here are a few success stories and the principles upon which they are based:

—*Love the product.* Employees work harder when they love their jobs or the products they make or the services they deliver, according to Alessandra Bianchi writing in *Inc.* "Survey after survey shows that employees today want to feel good about what they do; they want to feel they are making a contribution to society."

Her article is illustrated by an employee named Monette Paparotti who works for a bicycle helmet manufacturer in California and who also bicycles. Paparotti states: "When you believe in the product, [work] doesn't stop at the office."[14]

Good professors know all about loving the product: the minds of students. Undergraduates can invigorate us, even ones who openly challenge us in the classroom. They keep us sharp and current as much as any CD-Rom program or education seminar. We feel honored to teach such students and they know it.

—*Celebrate employees' outside interests.* Another article in *Inc.* highlights the owner of a Philadelphia cafe who accepts the fact that her employees have hobbies or dreams or other ambitions. "[I]nstead of resenting those outside interests," writes author Michael P. Cronin, "Wicks celebrates them. At the cafe's annual Anniversary Howl, employees exhibit their art, read their poetry, explain their volunteer work, and introduce their new babies."[15]

Case study: I'm a journalist who also happens to write poetry. So is ex-hostage/AP-bureau chief Terry Anderson whom I interviewed shortly after his release for *Writer's Digest.* The faculty at Oklahoma State University knew that poetry was one of my passions. Administrators there celebrated this, hosting readings at the school museum for me and honors tutorial students. They knew poetry didn't interfere with my journalism research but emphasized teaching and learning.

All professors have outside interests that define them as individuals. When appropriate, these should be acknowledged and encouraged because they help shape a professor's identity and sense of worth (too often homogenized in academe). Often such interests—book collecting to beekeeping—create a rich campus milieu and expose students to new intellectual passions or pursuits.

—*Fairness.* In many small businesses, this is a key word. In an article titled "Cashing In" and subtitled "Paying a lot is nice ... but it's paying wisely that matters most," Tom Ehrenfeld writes: "Pay alone does not qualify a company as a great place to work. If it were that easy, every company could just buy motivated employees. Nor are all good pay plans alike. Today they are varied as the ways in which companies are reorganizing their work."[16] Here are a few featured companies in that article and why they were cited:

1. Ashton Photo of Salem, Oregon, lets employees determine skills needed for various jobs, evaluate efficiency, and reward those who can teach others.

[Many faculties help determine profiles for positions and evaluate each other on merit committees, but too few emphasize fairness by rewarding professors who help each other, improving morale in the workplace.]

2. Aspect Telecommunications of San Jose, California, aligns pay with customer satisfaction and measures this with surveys and other quality-control factors.

[These innovations also relate to academe in as much as professors—especially those engaged in research—should be rewarded when they place their students in internships, jobs, or graduate schools. Exit and alumni surveys also could help gauge "customer" satisfaction.]

3. Calvert Group of Bethesda, Maryland, pays hidden costs spent by employees and even provides free running shoes for ones who walk to work.

[Career teachers have hidden costs—books and conferences, to cite only two—and researchers have more, from equipment and supplies to utility bills in home laboratories and offices. Even if universities reimburse professors for 10% of non-tax-deductible costs, the token gesture would lead to increased morale and productivity, as it often does in business.]

Some small companies, like Tom's of Maine, have expanded to midsize status because of another element: values.

Tom Chappell, president of a personal-care products company founded in 1970, promotes corporate values that apply directly to academe. I recommend his book, *The Soul of a Business: Managing for Profit and the Common Good* (Bantam, 1993), for educators, business people, and legislators interested in how personal and spiritual values can enhance morale and productivity. Here are values from an excerpt on managing autonomy, the section that most applies to the autonomous academic world, with my insertions in brackets:

—Define your corporate [read: educational] values; make them operate in decisions.

—Teach your employees to think, reason, and act in responsible relation to others— customers [students], fellow workers [professors], bosses [administrators], community [staff workers and citizens], and the environment [campus].

—Listen, reflect, share, and clarify. Job roles should be clearly defined. Whenever confusion arises, talk about it.

—Build diverse points of view into the process of setting goals and objectives. Encourage dialogue, welcoming differences of opinion. Diversity also belongs in your formalized systems of accountability.

—Use authority to guide, clarify, and affirm the power of others. Also use it to modify behavior that is controlling, domineering, or manipulative—or terminate it, if necessary.[17]

These business values adapt easily to higher education and help define the role of the manager in academe (also government). Peter F. Drucker speaks eloquently about this topic in "The Rise of the Knowledge Society." He states that good management is needed in all modern organizations. "In fact, we soon learned that it is needed even more in organizations that are not businesses. ... They need management the most precisely because they lack the discipline of the bottom line."[18]

The role of the manager has evolved as knowledge has become more important in society. Drucker states that the word "manager" once meant a person who was responsible for the work of subordinates. That changed in the 1950s when a manager identified a person who was responsible for the performance of employees.

Now this, too, has become too narrow a definition, he argues, maintaining "a manager is responsible for the application and performance of knowledge."[19]

What better definition than this to define an administrator? This passage from Drucker's essay emphasizes why good professors and courageous administrators should work together to change and improve higher education: "Intellectuals need their organization as a tool; it enables them to practice their technique, their specialized knowledge. Managers see knowledge as a means to the end of organizational performance. Both are right. They are poles rather than contradictions. Indeed, they need each other. The intellectual's world, unless counterbalanced by the manager, becomes one in which everybody 'does his own thing' but nobody does anything. The manager's world becomes bureaucratic and stultifying without the offsetting influence of the intellectual."[20]

In conclusion, it is possible to improve merit and morale in academe by adapting and incorporating business models into the structure of higher education. Administrators and professors should take the initiative, however, without interference from state government whose members often link education reform to their own short-term interests and agendas. Moreover, after merit models have been incorporated into academe, administrators and professors should analyze their short-and long-term effects and have the courage to improve upon or eliminate reforms that undermine morale or traditional educational values.

The good professor and the courageous administrator can set the standard again. They do not need government or business to do that for them, nor do they require a new building dedicated to effective teaching and a high-budget support staff endowed by industry. They need to implement ideas that reawaken their passions and that rankle the comfortable hierarchy.

In upcoming chapters, we'll encounter some of these ideas.

NOTES

1 "TQM: A Time for Ideas," by Ted Marchese, *Change*, May/June 1993, p. 13.
2 "Increasing Quality on Campus: What Should Colleges Do About the TQM Mania?" by George Keller, *Change*, May/June 1992, p. 49.
3 "The Rise of the Knowledge Society," by Peter F. Drucker, *Wilson Quarterly*, Spring 1993, p. 61.
4 Citations in this section are drawn from pages 10-13 of Ted Marchese's article in the May/June 1993 edition of *Change*.
5 "Corporate America's New Lesson Plan," by Lori Bongiorno, *Business Week*, 25 October 1993, p. 102.
6 Keller, 49.
7 Keller, 50.
8 "Colleges Should Not Be Blinded By Vision," by Richard Chait, *The Chronicle of Higher Education*, 22 September 1993, p. B2.
9 "New Approaches To Management Boosts Morale and Improves Financial Health at U. of Denver," by Goldie Blumenstyk, *The Chronicle of Higher Education*, 15 September 1993, p. A35.
10 Bongiorno, pp. 104-05.
11 "Gain-Sharing Report," by Tom Ehrenfeld, *Inc.*, August 1993, p. 87.
12 Ehrenfeld, 87.
13 "Trouble at the Top," by Amy Saltzman, *U.S. News & World Report*, 17 June 1991, pp. 40-41.
14 "True Believers," by Alessandra Bianchi, *Inc.*, July 1993, p. 72.
15 "One Life to Live," by Michael P. Cronin, *Inc.*, July 1993, p. 56.
16 "Cashing In," by Tom Ehrenfeld with additional reporting by Christopher Caggiano, *Inc.*, July 1993, pp. 69-70.
17 Tom Chappell, *The Soul of a Business* (New York: Bantam, 1993), p. 178.
18 Drucker, 68.
19 Drucker, 69.
20 Drucker, 70.

PART TWO

RAINBOW OF RESPONSES

==

Six

HYBRID STUDIES

We might as well admit that well-versed as our best methodologists have become, we
have yet to be able to predict much based on the studies we have done. ...
SAM G. RILEY, writing in *Journalism Educator*

INTRODUCTION

As mentioned earlier, I coined the term "academic socialism" while
I was a journalism professor at Oklahoma State University. The
economy in that state crashed in the early 1980s, causing several years
of hardship in higher education. During this period, no emphasis was
placed on merit because no money existed to reward it.

Many families suffered, including my own. Because Stillwater was
a university town, isolated to the west and north of Tulsa and

Oklahoma City, housing prices dropped dramatically. The ranch home that we purchased in 1983 for $50,000 sank in value to $35,000 by 1986. Like other property owners, we had little equity. To sell our home meant we would have to pay our Savings and Loan the difference between two mortgages, plus costs, or more than $11,000. At least I had tenure and a job. Some professors who normally would have received tenure were denied it (to meet budget cuts) and so were not replaced. Some released professors had bought houses and lost everything.

Morale at the university was critically low. Everyone wanted to be somewhere else, it seemed, but were "house-bound" at OSU. Professors were at the mercy of the Legislature because they could not move away without also declaring bankruptcy. In essence, the Legislature (responsible for poor planning that contributed to the bad economy) and the business sector (responsible later in part for the Savings and Loan scandal) could hammer at education, unscathed.

By 1985, I had composed a draft of my essay "Academic Socialism." It eased some of the stress to vent about lack of merit and low morale in academe. It pained me to see professors with hitherto pristine credit ratings lose houses to Savings and Loans. My wife Diane and I let our S&L foreclose on our house and relocated to Ohio University in Athens. We rented a cedar house on a ridge in the foothills of the Appalachian mountains, far from the plains and buttes of north central Oklahoma.

Like a brush fire, the bad economy was working its way north.

At OU, I gave a copy of my essay to Guido Stempel, editor of *Journalism Quarterly* and a distinguished professor in our field. I had known about him and respected him for years. Stempel, in fact, had published my first scholarly research study—"Periodicals Publishing More About Journalism Education." Coincidentally, a part of my 1975 study analyzed the relationship between business and academe, recommending that professors listen to "expressed concerns about what is good and bad about present-day journalism education. ..." Thus, in some sense, I have been analyzing this relationship on and off for almost 20 years. When I came to Stempel in 1986, asking him to critique a draft of my essay, he suggested revisions and clarifications.

For instance, he pointed out to me the fact that departmental raise pools were more or less allocated across-the-board without regard to excellence. I revised the essay and sent it to Stanley W. Lindberg, editor of *The Georgia Review,* who asked for a revision incorporating or rebutting the philosophies of E.D. Hirsch and Allan Bloom whose respective books *Cultural Literary* and *The Closing of the American Mind* were rising as bestsellers. I did as Lindberg requested and sent the essay to him late in 1987. By now, however, outside readers at Lindberg's magazine believed that Hirsch and Bloom had set the agendas for the debate about education reform, focusing more on cultural influences concerning academe than on administrative accountability. Finally, in the summer of 1991, almost six years after I had composed the first draft of "Academic Socialism," it was accepted by Dr. James B.M. Schick, editor-in-chief of *The Midwest Quarterly,* who again suggested revisions and clarifications. One dissenting reader on the MQ editorial board had criticized the qualitative approach, suggesting that it contained "half-truths ... all on the side of angels, of course." Another reader stated: "I, for one, grow weary of people who complain about the need for good teaching and who provide no clues about what this means, or how, in practical terms, teachers are to be evaluated."

No longer needing to "vent," I toned down the voice of my piece and did more research, revising according to Schick's suggestions. But the dissenting comments stayed with me when I decided to write a book based on the essay appearing in Fall 1992 edition of *The Midwest Quarterly.* Now a full professor, I had my doubts about qualitative and quantitative research. It seemed that the former massaged footnotes, using ones to support theses and omitting ones that refuted them, and the latter massaged figures, using ones to support hypotheses and omitting ones that refuted them. Worse, qualitative studies seemed to succeed in large part because of the caliber of writing—which has more to do with language skills than with truths. The stronger the writing, the better the argument. An essayist can win a case as an attorney does in court, relying solely on the ability to argue, circumventing justice. Likewise, quantitative studies generally lack the cogent arguments of qualitative counterparts and/or comments and opinions of respondents that shape arguments and often determine outcomes of issues.

In truth, numbers provide narrow views that often are subject to interpretation. Now the researcher's opinions color the data much like the essayist's opinions color the footnotes. The difference, however, lies in the fact that it is relatively easy to reject the essayist's opinions with a well-penned letter to the editor. Not so when it comes to numbers, often requiring exhaustive studies to test, rebut, or refute conclusions of a previous study. Thus, quantitative methods generally are accepted as more valid than qualitative ones.

Again, journalist Sam G. Riley puts this into perspective: "Even in a basically word-intensive area of study such as our own, numbers have become more honorific than words. Mere words are suspect; the use of numbers generates trust. ... We might as well admit that well-versed as our best methodologists have become, we have yet to be able to predict much based on the studies we have done—witness the considerable number of works with the word 'Toward' appearing in the head of their titles, which has always struck me as a tacit admission of at least partial defeat. My point is not that we should abandon our efforts in quantitative studies, but that the word, as opposed to the number, must come back into its own in importance if we are to aspire to real sophistication. ..."[1]

It is in that spirit that I have designed a hybrid study that attempts to attain such sophistication. In sum, an issue as far-reaching as educational reform is too important to rest solely on my ability to argue persuasively as an essayist or to interpret as a social scientist. True, an attorney might be able to sway a jury and win a case because of skillful oratory, but the judge and jury hear all sides. The essayist usually only presents one side of the debate, calls one set of witnesses, makes closing arguments and passes judgment. Conversely, the researcher presents numbers indicating a type or slice of reality, but unless those numbers are accompanied by attitudes, arguments, and opinions, they may lack clout or significance.

Thus, I have segmented this book into two parts. Already I have put forth my case qualitatively in the first five chapters, called my own set of witnesses, rebutted a few opposing arguments, and made a persuasive closing statement. Now it is time to test my arguments and hear what others in business, education and government have to say.

Then I'll present their conclusions and my recommendations to you, a jury of readers.

Only you can decide the outcome of this case.

DESIGN OF SURVEY

I designed a survey (or actually three surveys with slight variations) to obtain ideas and opinions from select groups in business, education, and government. The survey would test assumptions made in my original essay as published in *The Midwest Quarterly*. Those assumptions are found in the first five chapters of this book.

Survey results were not meant to depict the university as it exists factually. Those interested in such data should consult the myriad studies published in *The Chronicle of Higher Education Almanac* issue.

My surveys were meant to be basic in many respects. I would ask respondents to react to 10 statements to test 10 hypotheses. I would word statements as simply as possible so that respondents would feel the need to comment and clarify their positions on the back of surveys. In letters sent to select groups of business people and educators, I would summarize my essay in *The Midwest Quarterly* and encourage comments with this sentence: "Feel free to write additional comments on the back or even a personal letter if you feel strongly about any issue covered or *not* covered in the survey." The select government group received an accompanying letter that did not summarize tenets of my essay but that explained that I was "researching the issues of merit and morale in higher education." They were also advised: "Finally, feel free to write a personal letter if you feel strongly about any issues covered or not covered in the survey. You may also send any data or publications that you have compiled and that may be useful in my research." In addition, each survey contained this note: "If you feel strongly about any issue covered in this survey (or not covered), please use the reverse side to comment."

The survey was meant to measure attitudes and elicit opinions about the relationship of business and education, tenure, evaluation methods, and merit and morale (among other issues). To do so, some statements were worded according to the group at which they were aimed. For instance, the business group was asked to respond to this statement: "Employees of lower rank should evaluate their managers." The education group was asked: "Professors of lower rank should evaluate department heads." (Each individual survey will appear in chapters on the business, educator, and government responses.) In essence, statements 1-6 on the survey were identical for all groups. Statements 7 and 10 were identical for the educator and government groups with variations in the business survey to correlate with that group. Questions 8 and 9, however, were worded differently for each group to test specific attitudes: the concept of "teamwork" in business, morale of lower-rank professors, and accountability in government. Nonetheless, combined responses for these statements were tabulated to show a general view of the role of authority and rank in evaluation procedures of select groups. Here is the survey model:

COLLAPSED SAMPLE SURVEY

Circle the appropriate number under each question below:
1=Strongly Agree 2=Agree 3=Neutral 4=Disagree 5=Strongly Disagree
1. The business and education worlds operate on similar principles.

  1   2   3   4   5

2. I think the current educational system needs to be improved.

  1   2   3   4   5

3. I think merit (reward for good work) is important in business.

  1   2   3   4   5

4. I think merit is important in education.

  1   2   3   4   5

5. I think tenure (continual reappointment, with few stipulations) is an important aspect of higher education.

  1   2   3   4   5

6. Benefits (unemployment/severance pay) create a kind of tenure for executives with seniority in the business world.

  1   2   3   4   5

7. The best and worst senior [employees, professors] should be funded equally, according to rank.

  1   2   3   4   5

8. [Employees, professors] of lower rank should evaluate [each other's, senior professors'] job performance to determine pay scale and promotion.

    1   2   3   4   5

9. [Employees, professors] of lower [and upper=*government only*] rank should evaluate their [managers, department heads].

    1   2   3   4   5

10. [Executives, administrators] should bolster morale when forced to make cutbacks.

    1   2   3   4   5

Originally, the educator group was asked two additional questions concerning raise pools and administrative salaries. These were eliminated from the study after five respondents questioned the wording of these statements, indicating that other respondents might misinterpret them.

GROUP SELECTION

Select groups consisted of business leaders from the corporate, midsize, and small-business sectors; educator-writers from public and private universities; and governor's education aides. Here is a summary of how respondents in each group were selected:

Business Group

Names of 15 respondents were provided by colleagues in the Journalism School at Ohio University, representing leaders in large and midsize communications companies. I chose another five names from the publishing sector. An additional 25 names came from lists compiled by the Ohio University Alumni Foundation, representing small-business leaders interested in higher education issues. Some 25 surveys were sent to executives in Japan, Korea, and the Republic of China because of their emphasis on service and quality and/or global markets. (These leaders were asked specifically to share merit models that might be adapted to academe.) The remaining 130 names came from *Reference Book of Corporate Managements, Black Enterprise: 25 Top Black Investment and Financial Leaders, Fortune 500 Compact-*

Disclosure CD-Rom, America's Corporate Families, and *Corporate Yellow Book.*

Educator Group

Educator names came from the 1992-93 edition of *A Directory of American Poets and Fiction Writers* (Poets & Writers, Inc.) Names with university addresses were identified. From these, 175 nationally known writers were chosen, mostly from English departments, with the remaining 25 respondents coming from the humanities or specifically selected by me (to include noted writers and essayists). No preference was given to public or private schools and between 3-5 names were chosen from each of 50 states.

Government Group

Governor's education aides in each of 50 states, representing an entire universe, were chosen from listings in *The Chronicle of Higher Education Almanac.* When a state listed the position as vacant, government agencies were contacted and the name and address of the aide in question was procured.

These groups were targeted for their potential to provide opinions. In sum, it is the opinion of educators that dictate morale in an academic unit or university. The opinions of these particular educators—many of them nationally known as poets and essayists—give them added power as truth-tellers and foils. Although they do not represent a cross-section of disciplines in academe, almost all teach in colleges of Arts & Sciences, which typically include disciplines ranging from astronomy to zoology and from Arab to Zulu cultural studies. As for business leaders, their opinions can influence curricula, endowments, scholarships, and legislatures. The opinions of education aides inform governors who appoint regents that oversee many universities or who set education agendas, influencing the culture and/or administration of private colleges.

While results of surveys sent to the business, educator, and governor's aide groups do not claim to be representative of the business, education, and government sectors in the statistical sense, they are indicative of those populations. Unlike a general population survey, where researchers try to generalize from a sample to determine the attitudes of specific populations, this hybrid study takes a more general approach by tapping informed opinions of these diverse groups of leaders. Given these populations, the results of each study are important in at least three ways: In and of itself, as a foil to my own qualitative opinions, and in comparison to each other.

Finally, the business survey was sent 1 June 1993. The educator and governor's aide surveys were sent 1 October 1993. In any case, more than 75% of the research was completed for the qualitative section of this book before the business surveys were sent. More than 95% of the research was completed by the time the remaining surveys were sent. The qualitative sections were complete by the time the final survey was received in mid December 1993.

METHODS OF ANALYSES

Research assistants measured statistically the attitudes of three select groups on the following issues, probed in the first five chapters of this book: business and education comparison, quality of education, merit, tenure, seniority, reward principles, evaluation procedures, accountability, and morale.

A five-point Likert scale was used to measure 10 statements. Respondents were asked to circle the appropriate number which represented their agreement to each question as illustrated in the sample survey above. The lowest value was given to choices representing the respondent's most favorable attitude toward each statement; the highest value represented the respondent's least favorable attitude toward each statement. Respondents were told the study concerned issues of merit and morale in higher education and were asked twice—in accompanying letters and on surveys—to comment about any issue covered or not covered in the study. Permission to use respondents' names was also asked.

The survey was designed with simple statements on one page so as not to impose heavily on the respondent's time. This was particularly important in that only one mailing would be made to each group with no follow-up postcard or telephone call to non-respondents. (In a loose sense, the percentage response would not only indicate interest in higher education on the part of business but also gauge commitment on the part of educators and governor's aides.) Statistical analysis of each set of surveys was used to discover facts or tendencies relating to each groups' response to each question and the combined overall response to each question. For example, research assistants considered such issues as: Do governor's education aides view tenure favorably? Are the aides' views on tenure closer to that of business or more like that of education?

Statistical procedures were meant to generate a numerical data pool. The data, however, draw meaning only when applied to the hypotheses and parameters of this study. The statistical methods used here are simple tools to enhance the reader's knowledge of the select issues above and to compel business leaders, educators, and legislators to investigate and act upon problems of merit and morale in academe.

Statistical procedures used to analyze the data were frequency counts (head count), group mean scores (the arithmetic average), valid percents (calculated by way of actual response instead of total response) and Oneway Analysis of Variance (to pinpoint any significant difference between each group's response to a particular question).

Each question was analyzed for group response and also for combined group response. For example, how did educators perceive the idea of tenure? How did all respondents (business leaders, educators, governor's education aides) view the idea of tenure?

The Oneway Analysis of Variance (ANOVA) was run on each question to see if there was a significant difference in attitude among each of these different groups representing business, higher education, and government. If any significance was found, a Post Hoc test was run to pinpoint which group differed in agreement from the other groups. In sum, the ANOVA tells us there is a significant difference between groups and the Post Hoc test shows us where that difference exists.

HYPOTHESES

These hypotheses were drawn from the qualitative section of this book, subtitled "Making My Case":
1. Respondents from the three groups would tend to disagree that the business and academic worlds operate on similar principles.

2. Respondents from the three groups would tend to agree that higher education needs to be improved.

3. Respondents from the three groups would tend to agree that merit is important in business.

4. Respondents from the three groups would tend to agree that merit is important in education.

5. Business and government respondents would tend to disagree that tenure is an important academic concept.

6. Educators would tend to agree that tenure is an important academic concept.

7. Educators would tend to agree that executive seniority creates a kind of tenure system in the business world.

8. Educators would differ significantly from business and government respondents in perceiving how the evaluation process rewards merit.

9. Business respondents who commented on the back of survey would share their methods of rewarding merit.

10. Educators who commented on the back of surveys would share their comments about morale in academe.

NOTES

1 "Faculty Bashing: Some Implications for Mass Communication Professors," by Sam G. Riley, *Journalism Educator*, Autumn 1993, pp. 68-69.

Seven

THE BUSINESS RESPONSE

Educators are underpaid and until salaries and other benefits are equal to those in business, you will not attract or retain good people in the education process.

THOMAS McKEON, Vice President, Citicorp Center, Taiwan, Republic of China

RESPONDENTS

The return rate for the business group was 25%, or 49 out of 200. Twenty-nine business leaders had comments, with 17 of these agreeing to use of their names. For the most part, the respondents discussed such issues as the business-education relationship, tenure, merit, and morale.

FINDINGS

Here is the survey that select business people received with tabulated percentages under each of the five responses of the Likert scale: Circle the appropriate number under each question below:
1=Strongly Agree 2=Agree 3=Neutral 4=Disagree 5=Strongly Disagree
1. The business and education worlds operate on similar principles.

Strongly Agree	Agree	Neutral	Disagree	Strongly Disagree
2.1%	12.8%	12.8%	40.4%	31.9%

2. I think the current educational system needs to be improved.

Strongly Agree	Agree	Neutral	Disagree	Strongly Disagree
57.1%	32.7%	2.0%	4.1%	4.1%

3. I think merit (reward for good work) is important in business.

Strongly Agree	Agree	Neutral	Disagree	Strongly Disagree
69.4%	20.4%	0.0%	2.0%	8.2%

4. I think merit is important in education.

Strongly Agree	Agree	Neutral	Disagree	Strongly Disagree
55.1%	30.6%	6.1%	2.0%	6.1%

5. I think tenure (continual reappointment, with few stipulations) is an important aspect of higher education

Strongly Agree	Agree	Neutral	Disagree	Strongly Disagree
6.1%	22.4%	10.2%	32.7%	28.6%

6. Benefits (unemployment/severance pay) create a kind of tenure for executives with seniority in the business world.

Strongly Agree	Agree	Neutral	Disagree	Strongly Disagree
4.1%	24.5%	6.1%	57.1%	8.2%

7. The best and worst senior employees in my company should be funded equally, according to rank.

Strongly Agree	Agree	Neutral	Disagree	Strongly Disagree
2.1%	6.3%	4.2%	27.1%	60.4%

8. Employees of lower rank in my company should evaluate each other's job performance to determine pay scale and promotion.

Strongly Agree	Agree	Neutral	Disagree	Strongly Disagree
0.0%	16.7%	6.3%	35.4%	41.7%

9. Employees of lower rank should evaluate their managers.

Strongly Agree	Agree	Neutral	Disagree	Strongly Disagree
2.1%	39.6%	25.0%	22.9%	10.4%

10. Executives should bolster morale when forced to make cutbacks.

Strongly Agree	Agree	Neutral	Disagree	Strongly Disagree
40.9%	38.6%	11.4%	0.0%	9.1%

In sum, nearly three-fourths of the business respondents disagree or strongly disagree that the business and education worlds operate on similar principles. Only 15% agree that the two systems operate according to like tenets. Another 13% are neutral on the issue.

Most respondents (90%) strongly agree or agree that the current educational system needs to be improved. Only 8% disagree or strongly disagree with this perception.

An overwhelming 90% of the respondents strongly agree or agree that reward for good work is an important business component. Almost as many (86%) strongly agree or agree that merit is important in academe.

Most business respondents (61%) disagree or strongly disagree that tenure is important to higher education. Nearly 29% agree or strongly agree that tenure is important (but of these, only about 6% had a "strong agreement" feeling on the matter). Ten percent had no definite opinion on tenure.

Most of the business respondents (65%) disagree or strongly disagree that unemployment/severance pay creates a kind of tenure for executives with seniority. Over one-fourth (27%) feel that indeed unemployment/severance pay for executives with seniority is a kind of tenure. However, although some see the two employment practices in a similar way, the majority make no such connection.

Overwhelmingly, 88% disagree or strongly disagree that good and bad professors should be funded equally across-the-board. Only eight percent agree to the concept of equal pay for unequal contributions. This reconfirms that merit is highly prized by members of this group.

Concerning evaluation procedures, business respondents disagree or strongly disagree with the idea that lower-rank employees should evaluate each other to determine pay scale and promotion. Over three-fourths (77%) reject this practice. However, the combined attitude toward lower-rank employees evaluating their managers—no mention of raise or promotion in this question—is split: Over 40% agree with this idea, some 33% disagree, and about 25% have no opinion.

Business respondents overwhelmingly (80%) agree or strongly agree that executives should bolster morale when forced to make cutbacks. Only 9% strongly disagree with this statement.

GROUP COMMENTS

Several of the 29 business respondents who provided comments addressed two or more issues. In sum, there were five comments about the business-education relationship, five about tenure, eighteen about merit, three about morale, and a few on topics not related to the survey.

"I don't have time to complete your survey," wrote the owner of a midsize Ohio manufacturing company. This response may explain the low overall return rate for this group. In fact, some corporations have eliminated responding to surveys altogether or respond only to ones associated with their products or services.

Here is the text of a letter received from The Quaker Oats Company, sent by its media relations coordinator: "I appreciate your interest in The Quaker Oats Company by the submission of your questionnaire. However, each year, the company receives a number of surveys. Even though it may only take a few minutes to respond to your questionnaire, it would take a significant amount of time to complete each one, and our staff is lean.

"While your area of study is important to us, it becomes very difficult to selectively determine which of the many worthy questionnaires to respond to. Therefore, we have refrained from responding to surveys. If you have any specific questions about Quaker or any of its products, please do not hesitate to call our Consumer Response group or myself.

"I hope your research goes well."

The polite text has a mailmerge feel to it. I also received similar letters from the Campbell Soup Company and the Marriott Corporation.

Nonetheless, several top executives of major corporations took time to reply to the survey and make comments.

The chief executive of a U.S. defense contractor believed that higher education, particularly private institutions, were really businesses at the core. "However," he wrote, "most of the academics who teach either can't or won't accept this fact. As a result, there is little concern as to who the real customer is (often the ignored undergraduate) and little attempt to get costs in line with the growth or lack thereof in the economy in general. ..." He added, "I'll predict that higher education will follow the health industry in being 'helped' by the U.S. government."

This CEO knows about government as much as any top executive in the United States, making his prediction particularly unsettling. It seems to underscore the observation in "Chapter Five" concerning merit models. Unless educators adapt and incorporate business practices into academe, government may do this for them by decree, perhaps damaging traditional educational values.

Another top executive of a major U.S. corporation has left business and joined the faculty of a prestigious university. His observations about the business-education relationship are important because he has only recently made the transition. "Having spent 17 years in business before I entered university teaching last year, I was astonished by some of the practices I saw prevalent in academia," he writes. "I feel that universities are at least twenty years behind the times in how they treat their employees." As for professors, the former executive adds, "I am also concerned by the lack of focus among faculty in producing a coherent training in their disciplines for undergraduates. At research-oriented universities especially, the focus of classroom teaching often seems conducted more for the benefit of the faculty than the students."

The owner of a McDonald's restaurant in Ohio echoed that concern. "It appears 'research' is given priority over teaching," he writes. "This method has to be questioned at any state-run college or university. Its purpose is to educate our young people and not make a name for either the prof or the university." He rebuts academe's standard response to that issue by adding, "I know many execs who earn less than a prof and put in 40 to 60 hours a week only to take home paper work every night."

The president of a midsize Indiana company seemingly has lost faith in academe. "It would be nice if the business world and the educational world did operate on similar principles of reward for accomplishment and success, but in education," he observes, "we lost it somewhere back when the little red schoolhouse disappeared."

This respondent also was one of five who in part blamed tenure for shortcomings in higher education. "No system, no organization, none of God's creatures could thrive, and most would not even survive, if the undesirables were not continually purged from the organization. Improved education will take place when and only when tenure is eliminated and the great teachers in our educational institutions are rewarded and encouraged."

Frederick Feirstein, a New York City psychoanalyst and writer known for his candid views, contributed this comment: "Tenure, instead of protecting freedom of speech, as it was meant to do, inhibits it." In light of political correctness, Feirstein says, the pressure to conform limits free speech of professors so that tenure has lost its purpose and now merely protects jobs.

"Tenure does far more to protect non-performers than it does to compensate for excellence," writes Gary C. Smith, president of an Ohio bank. "I am opposed to the entire concept of tenure, relative to protecting ineffective 'educators.'" Smith would replace tenure with an evaluation system that measures such issues as "How effectively are students absorbing the material and how pertinent to their fields of endeavor is the material itself?"

The president of a national telecommunications firm writes: "The only good thing about tenure is that it protects the incompetents. If tenure is good, why don't coaches get tenure?"

Thomas Carmody, president and chief executive officer of American Business Products in Atlanta, laments: "If I come back, I'd like to come back as a college professor under today's scenario—status, tenure."

No respondent made a comment in support of tenure, but more than two thirds of those with comments spoke about merit and morale in the workplace. Several shared methods that they thought would be useful in or somehow related to higher education.

The McDonalds owner who disliked tenure also spoke about how he deals with employees when forced to make cutbacks. "(Cutbacks) must be explained in a positive way so as to let everyone know they are being (instituted) out of necessity and not desire. Those still working must be made aware that productivity probably needs to be increased so more cutbacks are not necessary." He noted that his policy "might sound harsh, but this is the real world of private enterprise" and had this parting shot aimed at academics: "There are no taxpayers to pick up the slack."

Some respondents felt differently, and a few even saw a direct link between issues or merit and morale in business and education.

"This was a very hard survey to fill out for me," wrote a general manager of a major hotel chain. He acknowledged that merit is as difficult to achieve in his profession as in education. "I've been in the business world now 15 years and I have always been very vocal about compensation, its implementation, criteria and standards. I am, too, in an industry (hospitality) where compensation has been based for years on length of service and not on your performance and aptitude to perform the job. It is also or was a 'lowest paid' industry." Nonetheless, the respondent held himself accountable for the morale at his hotel. "I have always in my career done more with less because of my leadership and motivational abilities. In the business world, I have always managed with efficiency by combining jobs, using creative scheduling, and being sensitive to employee needs."

Thomas McKeon, a vice president at the Citicorp Center in Taiwan, wrote: "Educators are underpaid and until salaries and other benefits are equal to those in business, you will not attract or retain good people in the education process." McKeon believes the future of the United States rests on our educational values at all levels, grade school through graduate school. Moreover, he recommends specific measures to maintain morale during cutbacks:

—Provide open communication and career counseling to all employees.

—Establish clear paths to career opportunities even in times of cutbacks.

—Explain steps to be taken by management and staff to help individual employees achieve those objectives.

Pierson M. Grieve, chairman and CEO of Ecolab in St. Paul, a Fortune 500 company employing 11,000 people worldwide, shared similar beliefs:

—Explain why a cutback is necessary.

—Explain how the decision was made with regard to employees affected by the cutback.

—Provide those affected with "all the financial and moral support possible."

David J. Samuels, who recently retired as an executive of Ohio Bell Telephone, contributed these guidelines to maintain morale during tough economic times:

1. Let employees know why cutbacks are being made.

2. Identify and inform those employees involved in the cutbacks.

3. Establish a program for implementation of cutbacks and inform employees when they will occur.

4. If possible, identify and reassign employees to weather the cutbacks.

5. Establish retraining or job counseling at the company's expense and offer early retirement or other inducements to help implement the cutback program.

Above all, Samuels added, do not keep cutbacks secret or instill fear and blame in the workplace. "This is the quickest way to lower morale," he notes, explaining why executives should be held accountable during hard times. "Management would do well to make the process of cutbacks as pleasant as possible because those employees who are left will have long memories." According to Samuels, "People want to feel that they are being treated as adults in a fair and just manner. So even under adverse conditions, morale can be kept reasonably above average."

Lynette Wood, president of Wood Advertising in Chicago, echoed many of Samuels' suggestions. Executives should make clear that cutbacks and job performance are usually two distinct issues. Let employees know "they are good workers" and that "excellent references will be provided," she states. Then Wood recommends outplacement services for any employees let go during cutbacks. The company should provide help in the job search, back-up clerical support, and information on insurance and counseling. "Executives have a responsibility to be human when making cutbacks," she concludes.

This view was echoed by Carol S. Rosener, a training contractor for major corporations like Motorola. "The employee's perception of integrity accounts for so much," she writes. "If the executive communicates and listens openly and honestly—and takes part in the suffering and financial give-backs—these actions and trust will bolster morale for most."

Robert McDowell, co-founder of Story Line, a small-press in Oregon, thinks maintaining morale is important during good and bad economic times. "Attend to the quality of the inner life," McDowell recommends. If executives have to assign more responsibilities to employees during cutbacks, they can balance that by "making them feel not only like a team player, but more responsible to the team itself." McDowell suggests holding weekly staff meetings to promote team spirit and solve problems together.

"Keep up on the lives of employees," he says, "and remember birthdays, anniversaries. Be understanding about needed time off. Give gifts.

"The little things help."

Kathryn Britenriker-DeVeau, an assistant manager of a nationally known store chain, also believes in team spirit to maintain morale. "Cutbacks are like everything else and must be approached and conducted with a team effort, team mentality, for the good of the team.

Morale like motivation comes from within," she adds. "Executives are only able to provide the tools for associates to use."

Santiago Ruperez, representative of Banco Santander in Taipei, said he has been employing Zen methods of self-knowledge to help him grow as an executive and a person. "Reward and merit systems are bound to fail unless they are based upon the real foundations of the true self. If you encourage the vanity of your ego, you will bring disaster to your business, education, or your life. ... Once you know yourself, you can do as you please with the greatest results."

These other respondents had brief comments about merit and morale:

— "Communicate the reason for cutbacks and feed back to remaining employees the reason for their continued employment" (from David Shelton, executive director, manufacturing, Colgate Palmolive Company).

— "Employee feed back and participation are critical to performance" (from Thomas B. Boklund, CEO, Oregon Steel Mills).

— "Executives should always strive to motivate" (from the president of a national telecommunications company).

— "Outline future plans to remaining employees" (from a New York City television executive).

— "(Uphold morale) by speaking directly to each and every employee" (from Jim Cunningham, account executive, Dorna USA).

— "During cutbacks, employees should be given as much information as possible so that they are not in the dark during these stressful times" (from a top executive of a New York City financial firm).

— "Delegate to senior managers responsibility and involvement in how cutbacks are to be made, formulating strategies for change and improvement" (from the publisher of a small Ohio daily newspaper).

— "Explain why cuts are necessary and what the outcome will be if they are not put into effect" (from an Ohio small-business owner).

Finally, two executives provided comments indirectly associated with issues in the survey.

George R. Wackenhut, chief executive officer of the Wackenhut Corporation of Coral Gables, Florida, stated: "I am most concerned with the present failure of our public school system to prepare young people to become productive members of society. High schools seem to do a good job in preparing students for college. But what about those young people who are not college-bound?"

Edward Polen, president of Emco Chemical Distributors in North Chicago, Illinois, stated: "Let's not forget that America has existed under Capitalism and Democracy for over 200 years. We have become the greatest nation on earth under Capitalism and Democracy. Over the last few years we have become more divided as a people—those that have and those that have not. It is very unfortunate to be a have-not, yet, all men were not and are not created equal. Let's not destroy what got us here!"

CONCLUSIONS

Based on responses from select members of the business sector, these general conclusions can be drawn:

1. Business leaders disagree that the business and education worlds operate on the same principles.

2. Respondents believe that the current educational system needs to be improved.

3. An overwhelming majority of the respondents agree that reward for good work is an important business concept. Almost as many agree that merit in academe is important, too.

4. As a group, the respondents tend to view the issue of tenure unfavorably. Only a relative few of the respondents had no opinion on this matter. Less than a third of the respondents believed that tenure is important in higher education. But even this response was generally soft, with only about 6% in strong support of tenure. Conversely, a significant number of respondents (28.6%) indicate a strong dislike of tenure. This suggests that negative attitudes about tenure will be hard to change with many opinion-makers in the business sector.

5. Respondents disagreed that unemployment benefits and severance pay create a kind of tenure in the business sector. However, disagreement here was softer than this conclusion might indicate in as much as only about 8% of the respondents had a strong negative feeling about this comparison. This suggests that some aspects of the comparison were

valid but not all to the majority of respondents.

6. Respondents disagree that good and bad professors should be funded equally across-the-board, confirming their belief that higher education should prize merit as much as the business sector does.

7. Respondents do not believe that lower-rank employees should evaluate each other for raises and/or promotions. This suggests that business respondents feel that an executive should be evaluating lower ranks when money or power is involved.

8. Even when money and power issues are no longer a factor in the evaluation process, respondents have no significant feeling about lower-rank employees evaluating managers. However, a plurality of about 40% saw some usefulness in this idea. This suggests support of this method of evaluation for improvement's sake in the name, say, of teamwork or mission.

9. Respondents generally agree that executives should bolster morale when forced to make cutbacks. This supports the idea that executives are accountable for morale, especially during tough economic times. The 9% who strongly disagree with this concept may represent the hard-core Darwinian segment of the business world, which puts authority or profit margin or competition above the everyday concerns of employees. In reality, as this study shows, companies with such a management style probably constitute a small fraction of the business sector; however, this Dickensian stereotype still symbolizes business for many people in academe with no or little experience in business.

10. Here is a more accurate profile of the business leader, drawn from his or her opinions, as reflected by findings of the survey:

He or she feels that business and education operate on different principles, and the latter needs to be improved. The business leader identifies strongly with the concept of merit in business and in education and thinks that this should be reflected somehow in an employee's or a professor's paycheck or status. Nonetheless, the business person would probably do away with tenure in higher education and sees no similar component in business, even with executives who would be eligible for unemployment benefits and severance pay. The respondent dislikes the idea of lower-rank employees evaluating each other and feels a superior should be responsible for determining raises and/or promotions. Even when raises or promotions are not at stake, the respondent may also feel uncomfortable with the idea of lower-rank employees evaluating superiors but would probably allow it to improve teamwork or mission, however. When forced to make cutbacks, the business leader feels accountable for morale and tries to bolster it.

Eight

THE EDUCATION RESPONSE

It may be that some of our research priorities are misguided. There is too much emphasis on publication for its own sake, pushed mainly by the 'increased productivity' catchword. ... But the answer is not to make the university more like a factory, or more like a business. There, only the CEOs get to think.

PRICE CALDWELL, professor, Mississippi State University

RESPONDENTS

The return rate for the education group was 41.5%, or 83 out of 200. Thirty-seven educators had comments, with 23 of these agreeing to use of their names. For the most part, as in the business sample, respondents discussed such issues as the business-education relationship, tenure, merit, and morale.

FINDINGS

Here is the survey that select educators received, with tabulated percentages under each of the five responses of the Likert scale: Circle the appropriate number under each question below:
1=Strongly Agree 2=Agree 3=Neutral 4=Disagree 5=Strongly Disagree
1. The business and education worlds operate on similar principles.

Strongly Agree	Agree	Neutral	Disagree	Strongly Disagree
3.7%	23.2%	14.6%	41.5%	17.1%

2. I think the current educational system needs to be improved.

Strongly Agree	Agree	Neutral	Disagree	Strongly Disagree
43.9%	48.8%	4.9%	2.4%	0.0%

3. I think merit (reward for good work) is important in business.

Strongly Agree	Agree	Neutral	Disagree	Strongly Disagree
57.3%	37.8%	2.4%	1.2%	1.2%

4. I think merit is important in education.

Strongly Agree	Agree	Neutral	Disagree	Strongly Disagree
59.8%	34.1%	0.0%	3.7%	2.4%

5. I think tenure (continual reappointment, with few stipulations) is an important aspect of higher education.

Strongly Agree	Agree	Neutral	Disagree	Strongly Disagree
51.2%	34.1%	6.1%	6.1%	2.4%

6. Benefits (unemployment/severance pay) create a kind of tenure for executives with seniority in the business world.

Strongly Agree	Agree	Neutral	Disagree	Strongly Disagree
11.4%	16.5%	30.4%	30.4%	11.4%

7. The best and worst senior professors in my department should be funded equally according to rank.

Strongly Agree	Agree	Neutral	Disagree	Strongly Disagree
1.3%	2.6%	2.6%	34.6%	59.0%

8. Professors of lower rank (assistant, associate) in my department should evaluate senior professors' job performance to determine salary and promotion.

Strongly Agree	Agree	Neutral	Disagree	Strongly Disagree
7.3%	12.2%	15.9%	31.7%	32.9%

9. Professors of lower rank should evaluate department heads.

Strongly Agree	Agree	Neutral	Disagree	Strongly Disagree
28.0%	41.5%	11.0%	11.0%	8.5%

10. Administrators should bolster morale when forced to make cutbacks.

Strongly Agree	Agree	Neutral	Disagree	Strongly Disagree
46.3%	36.3%	16.3%	0.0%	1.3%

In sum, more than half of the respondents (58%) disagree or strongly disagree that the business and education worlds operate on similar principles. However, more than one fourth of respondents (26%) believe business and education do share such principles. About 15% are neutral on the issue.

There is overwhelming agreement or strong agreement (93%) with the statement about the educational system needing to be improved. Only 5% are neutral and 2% disagree on this point. No respondent strongly disagrees.

The educators also agree or strongly agree (95%) that reward for good work is an important business concept. Only 2% have no opinion on the matter and another 2% disagree or strongly disagree.

Respondents again overwhelming agree or strongly agree (94%) that merit is important in education. No respondent is neutral on this statement and about 6% disagree or strongly disagree.

Respondents also support tenure, with 85% agreeing or strongly agreeing with the survey statement. Only 8% disagree or strongly disagree that tenure is an important aspect of higher education. Six percent are neutral on this issue.

However, respondents do not see a strong connection between tenure and business benefits (unemployment/severance pay). A significant 30% are neutral and a combined 42% disagree or strongly disagree with the comparison. However, some 28% of educators think the comparison is valid.

Educators overwhelming disagree or strongly disagree (94%) with the practice of funding good and bad senior professors equally, according to rank. This response confirms the earlier belief that merit is important in academe. In addition, it indicates that professors prefer achievement rather than seniority as a way to determine salary. Only a combined 4% agree or strongly agree with equal pay for unequal work.

On questions involving the evaluation process, most respondents (65%) disagree or strongly disagree that lower-rank professors should participate in the salary and promotion decisions of senior professors. Only about 20% of the sample approve of the idea and 16% are neutral.

However, the reverse is true when it comes to lower-rank professors evaluating department heads, with almost 70% in agreement or strong agreement. About 20% disagree or strongly disagree with this idea, and 11% are neutral.

A significant 83% believe that administrators should bolster morale when forced to make cutbacks, with 1% in disagreement. About 16% are neutral on this issue.

GROUP COMMENTS

Many of the 37 educators who provided comments addressed two or more issues. In sum, there were 12 comments about the business-education relationship, 9 about tenure, 9 about merit, 15 about morale, a few on topics not related to the survey and several short responses to individual questions.

As I suspected, many in this particular sample of educators—a group, by and large, known for its ability to express ideas—presented eloquent and powerful arguments. Thus, when possible, I will reprint their comments at length—a few are quite elaborate—without too much interruption or gatekeeping. However, to adjust for this, I have excluded a few minor comments by other educators—often only a phrase or two alongside a survey question—on an issue already covered in depth by previous respondents.

As indicated above, the second most popular topic in the comments section of the survey was the business-education relationship. Respondents mostly discussed differences between the two sectors.

Carol Muske, an English professor at University of Southern California, wrote: "I don't agree that education is a 'business' and should be treated as such. Universities seem inundated with administrators filled with business acumen who have created a 'top-heavy' over-salaried situation for themselves. Education indeed needs an overhaul from top to bottom in this country—but restructuring it after the model of the corporation seems a terrible, cynical idea.

"In my daughter's fifth grade, teachers have set up classrom 'corporations' and a 'pay for performance' milieu, with 'money' paid out as 'incentive' to the children to learn. All my daughter has learned from this is that if you have enough money, you can buy anything—not exactly the lesson I sent her off to learn."

Barbara Smith, chair of the Division of Humanities at Alderson-Broaddus College in Philippi, West Virginia, wrote: "The major differences between business and education are alluded to in your research project. It is relatively easy to evaluate performance in the strictly business world but not so easy in education. In business, an individual either 'produces' or does not. Also, customers know quite specifically what they want and need, and they 'measure' whether or not their desires and/or needs are met.

"Evaluation in education is another matter. For one thing, few customers know what they want or need beyond the obvious—jobs and security and something they've heard of but are sure they've never experienced—'fulfillment.' Futhermore, not all knowledge or learning can be accurately measured, and most knowledge and learning does not come from a single source such as a book or a class or a teacher or a school or a parent or a peer or a church. Even job placement, which is often used as the ultimate test of the effectiveness of an education, varies according to local as well as global markets and is therefore an unreliable measurement tool.

"At the same time that all of this is true, schools and colleges are increasingly being held accountable to the public in the same way that a corporation is accountable to its stockholders or a pizza palace is held accountable to its customers. As a result, evaluation processes have become more and more elaborate and more and more costly in time, dollars, and energy. And the results of the process are often misused. For example, research indicates that student evaluations are highly unreliable, but because the process of student evaluation is so labor and cost intensive, an inordinate amount of weight is attached thereto.

"As I indicated, education is being treated more and more as a business, and business practices are being applied. There are, indeed, strong similarities, and the application of business principles is revealing some of the very serious flaws in the administration and evaluation of education. However, we must bear in mind the critical differences between the two types of enterprise.

"In short, fruit is fruit, but apples are not oranges."

A professor from an Ohio college, who asked not to be identified, responded: "Of course education needs to be improved, but most of the issues raised here (on the survey) would be on the bottom of my list of how to do it. And asking if education needs improvement without asking if business does suggests a bias I am real uncomfortable with.

"Perhaps we are suffering more TQM at our institution than you are at yours, but I hate unqualified comparisons between business and education."

Bim Ramke, who teaches at the University of Denver, observed: "I have no expertise in the 'business world'—how can I know the answer to comparisons of business and education? But further— surely some principles of operation are similar, some different. The rest of the survey ignores the principle difference—students. We in education do not deal in commodities—we teach. But then there is research, and government contracts, and there are grants and administrative correspondence with funding agencies."

Three respondents had similar comments about the business-education relationship but also remarked about tenure.

A professor at an Illinois institution wrote that he could not identify himself because "it's my tenure review year, which means that I'm skittish and generally keeping to myself." On the other hand, he returned two single-spaced pages of comments.

Here is an excerpt: "I don't see the university as being any more cluttered with dead wood than the business world, where seniority and benefit plans and years to go before retirement weigh on the minds of any supervisor. Rather than tenure, which is job security, the business sector has a stronger union than the American Association of University Professors, which is more 'perk-oriented,' it seems, than AAUP, which is more freedom-oriented. But tenure does not guarantee that a professor will always have a job. If the professor commits any one of a variety of heinous crimes by faculty handbook standards, he or she can be dismissed—tenured or not. And if the university has to cut back on programs because of enrollment drops or funding cuts, positions can be cut and jobs terminated—again, tenured or not. All of which seems that tenure does, in fact, only guarantee one freedom of speech and freedom to teach."

"The system works this way," he continued. "In order to get tenure, junior faculty have to be active in three areas. They have to be the best teachers, they have to be most active on major campus committees, and they have to be among the most active in their chosen fields of scholarship/research. What this does, in effect, is wear down the junior faculty in a five-or six-year form of hazing, to where we all are quite unhappy campers. But how else can you get the university's business done? Youth is where the energy resides, and there is no carrot or stick quite like that of tenure and promotion which would do the trick."

The esteemed poet Richard Wilbur, professor emeritus of English at Smith College, believes the business and education worlds "are, or should be, competitive. But the goal of education is not financial profit." Wilbur adds that tenure is important "for the protection of free speech; otherwise, an evil."

Price Caldwell, a professor at Mississippi State University, carefully described the role of education in an excerpt that included a remark about tenure: "Universities should provide the imagination and conscience for the nation. Its role is not merely to be productive, i.e., part of the nation's industrial capacity.

"Tenure is not a ticket to a free ride. Teachers are motivated by their students. Most I know work damn hard. Tenure is a necessary protection for open thinking and writing, especially in these highly politicized times.

"It may be that some of our research priorities are misguided. There is too much emphasis on publication for its own sake, pushed mainly by the 'increased productivity' catchword. ... But the answer is not to make the university more like a factory, or more like a business. There, only the CEOs get to think."

Other respondents focused on the issue of tenure, providing brief pointed comments or extended analyses.

Alicia Ostriker, a professor in the English Department at Rutgers University in Newark, wrote: "I have found that tenure enabled me to do more risk-taking research than I otherwise would have dared to do. For others, it's a pillow."

A professor at a small South Carolina school who asked not to be identified wrote: "I agree with the basic premises of granting tenure, but I believe schools need to do a better job of evaluating and helping professors in their first two to three years of employment. By the end of the third year, a school should know if a particular faculty member is doing a good job or not, and if he isn't, the school should not string him along for another two to three years and then dump him."

David Curtis, a professor at Sacred Heart University in Fairfield, Connecticut, observed, "I have seen no indication that tenure changes a teacher's work habits. Tenure is not to my mind an employment issue; it is an academic freedom issue."

An emeritus professor of an Indiana university, who requested anonymity, linked arguments against tenure to cutbacks in education. "I believe that institutions of higher learning, even private schools, are in a bad way financially. I expect within a few years ... some sort of change in the way deans and presidents want to think about tenure. It wouldn't surprise me to see, eventually, some oxymoronic concept take over, such as 'renewable' tenure."

Leonard Trawick, a professor at Cleveland State University, believes "there is a false assumption that the purpose of tenure is primarily a benefit that rewards desired behavior—good teaching, publishing, dependability, etc. This is not the case: the purpose of tenure is to insure academic freedom: to protect a faculty member from being fired because of his or her ideas.

"There have been plenty of cases where tenure has provided this kind of protection: sometimes the offending ideas are political, but often departments are divided in intellectual conflicts, e.g., recently in my discipline, new critics vs. deconstructionists. I would not want my job to depend on having to tailor my teaching and writing to fit the dogmas of a doctrinaire department head."

Reg Saner, a professor at the University of Colorado, wrote alongside the survey question about tenure this intriguing remark: "PC tongue-lock completes the vanishing purpose of tenure." On the bottom of the survey he qualified that comment. "On tenure: a difficult question. My impulsive note, above, oversimplifies, I know, but. ...."

But Saner has a point. The more professors defend tenure on the grounds of "academic freedom" or "free speech," the more it seems threatened by the specter of political correctness.

Ron McFarland, a professor in the English Department at the University of Idaho, wrote: "I consider tenure to be at best a 'necessary evil,' and I'm not certain how necessary it is. In the 25+ years I've taught at the college level, I have generally observed that tenure sustains some of the worst and most mediocre of professors. No doubt it also protects some of the best and most outspoken, but I have never (personally) witnessed such a case."

As predicted, most respondents spoke about unfairness in academe and related it to morale.

This remark by Philip Dacey, an English professor at Southwest State University in Marshall, Minnesota, was so pointed that I used it as an epigraph to introduce Chapter Three on "Bad Attitudes": "Administrators should bolster morale when forced to make cutbacks by cutting administrators. Doing so would be a guaranteed morale-bolsterer."

The comment may sound flip, but several respondents echoed Dacey's putdown of administrators, focusing on accountability.

A nationally known, award-winning writer and English professor at a four-year research institution in the Southwest responded at length: "The administration (in academe) has become an empire unto itself. Salaries there are far in excess of those of faculty members, as is the power. This is unhealthy. Today, administrators, not faculty, set policy, and they do so without a system of checks and balances, without being held accountable for their actions.

"In my view, this has resulted in a situation not unlike that of the Church around the time of Martin Luther. Fat, aloof, not held accountable, 'professional' administrators have become a class of privileged, academic hustlers with little regard for the traditional purposes of their institutions.

"In this atmosphere, Political Correctness has become a convenient and, I might add, bloody, tool to promote administrators' own aggrandizement.

"Believe me, I do not enjoy sounding this negative, yet, given the prevailing situation, to voice a different opinion would be to fly in the face of reality. I say this, furthermore, after a long and continuing struggle with an administration that has blithely ruined the careers of colleagues who have tried to defend traditional values against popular fads.

"Perhaps in some way your researches can help counter what has become a destructive trend in American education."

This above respondent requested anonymity but did not ask me to conceal the identity of his or her institution. However, I decided to mask the name of the university in question because, I felt, specific remarks could be linked to the writer-professor. In another sense, it is unfortunate that the person feels that he or she must remain anonymous—probably because of a continuing morale problem with administrators—because the person's reputation in the literary world would add clout to the above arguments.

The comment of Peggy Shumaker, a professor at the University of Alaska-Fairbanks, appears in its entirety at the end of Chapter One as a representative statement from the educator group. "Here in Alaska," she writes, "increases are either across-the-board percentages or market-driven, both of which slight the humanities and arts, every time.

"Morale's awful."

An administrator at a small West Virginia college directed his comments in part at me. "I do believe in merit," he wrote. "At many small colleges people work very hard, teach many classes, and are expected to publish, etc., if they wish promotion. Most small colleges do not pay handsome salaries. How many classes do you teach, Professor Bugeja? How many students in those classes? What is your salary? Your concern is appreciated and I'm sure many of the 'crimes' you see in higher education are serious. However, in many small private schools they are not as real as they might be in large research universities, at least the tax-paying public is not gouged as much for fat cat, smug, lazy professors who are essentially frauds. ..."

For the record, I teach 275-285 students in ethics, magazine writing workshops, and independent studies (not counting summer school) per academic year. When an ethics class with an enrollment approaching 100 turns in final papers—this is in addition to exams and other assignments during the quarter—I bring home a box of some 1,000-1,500 individual pages to edit, analyze, and grade. This requires 40 hours over one week—final papers must be graded quickly to meet quarter deadlines—so I work several hours each day at home and all weekend. Moreover, each magazine writing workshop contains 14-22 students responsible for three drafts of articles and essays per quarter, representing about 600 individual pages that require editing and analysis in addition to marketing research. As for my salary, I was earning less than $40,000 per year when I was promoted to full professor at age 38. Now at 41 I earn $46,500 per academic year. In my 15 plus years as a professor at public four-year research institutions, I have never been assigned a teaching or research assistant, although one graduate student helped me five hours per week over the course of a quarter to compile lists of business persons included in this study and to print out letters and mail surveys. I do not know if I qualify as a fat cat, smug, lazy professor who essentially is a fraud—the respondent quipped "you and I, of course, are not among that odious group!"—but I do know that this stereotype is promoted by lawmakers and administrators with their own agendas and also contributes to low morale.

"You have the equation partly right. Morale is low," writes Charles Fishman, a professor in English/Humanities at SUNY-Farmingdale. "But the Peter Principle is a factor that you should factor in: many are promoted to positions above their competence where they do nothing or worse—while others who excel in their positions are systemically under-funded and under-supported." At the bottom of the page, Fishman added this postscript: "Further undermining of morale—and sanity—has occurred on this campus because our union has joined hands with administration, at the expense of faculty."

The following comment by eminent poet and writer Fred Chappell, a professor at the University of North Carolina-Greensboro, puts several merit and morale issues into crisp perspective: "Who is to judge the best teachers? We are told that students are untrustworthy, grading well those profs who give easy grades. One's colleagues have vested interests in putting one another down—or in pumping up their whole department. Administrators seem to think the university runs for their benefit and that the teachers and students are their natural enemies. Of course, UNCG may be a dreadful exception—but then why do I hear these same complaints at so many of the other schools I visit?

"There just seems to be no group or person to whom to turn as reliable judge and jury in the matter of teaching. It is a mighty subjective business. If one's students turn out well over the years, that's because you drew good material. If badly, because you drew bad.

"No wonder the administration turns to the publish-or-perish policy. But they have no sense about it. Here a guy who publishes a textbook gets as much credit as one who publishes a solid scholarly study. The profs are as proud of their committee work here as anything else, but they don't get much credit for that. Committees is a sucker's game. You work your butt off, turn in reports and recommendations to the administration, are given a pat on the head, more committee assignments, and no raise in pay. Nor tenure.

"It hasn't been a problem for me. Until the last few years (when I've become quite cranky) I've been a popular teacher and a pretty good one. And I've published great bunches of stuff, though alas not bunches of great stuff. Nothing much happened in my favor till some new administrator came in who wanted to make a mark for herself. She doubled my salary when I got the Bollingen Prize (pure luck, that) and made a lot of enemies doing so. But after 20 years in this joint I was making about $25,000 per annum.

"I take for granted that nobody knew what I was worth. Nor did I because I never knew what anyone else was making. Didn't care. Still don't except in the interest of rudimentary justice. But it's impossible for anyone to decide what is just in his own case. If we could be objective, we'd probably jail ourselves. ...

"So it's a mess," Chappell concluded. "If you can come up with solid suggestions for reform, I'd love to see them, although you're likely to meet the fate of all reformers. ... It's our good and earnest colleagues we worry about because they're got no protection except the reward of mediocrity that comes to all in the system."

David A. Evans, a widely published poet and professor at South Dakota State University, also criticized the system, believing that "seniority has disappeared from higher education or at least is fading fast. Professors who have achieved the rank of full prof should be respected more and given more money. Presumably," he noted, "they achieved their status by contributing to the profession."

Rabiul Hasan, adjunct instructor at Delgado Community College-City Park Campus in New Orleans, presented a different view of seniority. "A mere Ph.D. holder (without substantial publications) should not be given promotion and tenure regardless of the numbers of gray he has on his head. In some instances, these 'hollow' professors should be given 'pink slips,' thereby making room for instructors (alas! they don't have Ph.D.s) with impressive publications."

"A brilliant and well-published English professor can earn a great deal more than a less accomplished colleague but no more than an inferior business college faculty member," remarked another professor who asked not to be identified. He believes that teamwork and mission are undermined, along with morale, because of questionable budget decisions. "It's not that good teachers or good departments get the funding and support that they deserve, but that funding and resources are doled out in ways unrelated to a teacher's or department's success in meeting his/her professed goals."

Gary Fincke, a writer and professor at Susquehanna University in Pennsylvania, also observed that administrative priorities and faculty rewards often are not in sync in academe. "At Susquehanna, for instance, recruiting students is a high priority," he wrote, "yet those faculty who do recruit aren't rewarded."

Another professor who asked for anonymity believes the culture of an academic unit contributes to unfairness. "My 30 years in the academic community has been a paradox of extreme forms of dictatorship to a 'pure' sense of democracy (or socialism), neither of which is ideal—obviously.

"As a member of a department composed primarily of women—in an area that is usually seen as belonging to women—I'm intrigued with your study of socialism in the academy. You might want to look more closely at the constructs, especially the impact upon professionalism by women who see themselves as equal members of an academic department/community."

As illustrated in Chapter Four, women are an underclass in academe because of low starting salaries, not necessarily because of merit considerations.

Judith Kitchen, an adjunct professor at SUNY-Brockport, states: "I know that I will not receive the appointment I'd like not because of lack of merit, but because of too much of it. Those professors who are not publishing will not willingly let me into their ranks to become their direct rival for raises and honors, etc."

According to Kitchen, the culture of academe complicates the issue of merit. "The concept of equality enters the arena long before the professor is hired. We are supposed to look at our students as though they can each perform equally and that we must help some to achieve what comes naturally to others. We are not supposed to fail them, and they all—even those who hardly attend—are entitled to assess our abilities in the classroom. God forbid we should act as though some students are 'brighter' than others, that some might actually be 'better' as students, for whatever reasons a good student is a good student. The PC movement has seen to that. What if the good student were a white male? We might be considered racist or sexist. Better to pretend that they are all equally talented."

Merit also was on the mind of several other respondents.

One of the few to suggest methods to improve morale via merit was Elton Glaser, an English professor at the University of Akron. "I believe strongly that merit needs to be recognized in several ways in the university, particularly through salary increases, but also through other means, such as adjustment of work load and public recognition by administrators.

"Unfortunately, the recognition of merit is not likely to increase morale on campus because there are too many faculty who do too little that is worthy of merit. For such people, merit becomes a kind of code word for inequality and elitism and favoritism; they resent those professors who get the promotions and the raises and the reduced teaching loads.

"One answer is to institute a clearly understood system of incentives, so that good work—as a teacher or scholar or committee member—pays off in tangible ways. This system of rewards would put any recognition of merit on a fairly objective basis, and would lessen the resentment of mediocrities (though it will probably not make them any more effective as professionals)."

Joseph Duemer, a professor in the Center for Liberal Studies at Clarkson University in Potsdam, New York, believes: "Merit is important in education, but so is collegiality and the accommodation of merit. Marching solely under the flag of merit will, I fear, tend to narrow the range of differences we are capable of including within the free space of the imagination I think it is our job, as educators, to clear for our students and ourselves."

Duemer adds: "We've got to all be free to discuss ideas with each other, without the fear that we are being evaluated for next year's raise at the same time."

Another professor in the SUNY system who asked not to be identified said: "My complaint is that 'merit' is too often defined in academia as how much another institution is willing to pay one or what benefits another institution is willing to furnish one. It turns the teacher into a flirt."

Alongside a question about merit on the survey, Alicia Ostriker at Rutgers wrote: "What does happen, though, is that salary differentials are determined by the obtaining of outside offers—which correlates loosely with 'merit.'"

Two respondents had comments indirectly related to survey questions.

Lenard D. Moore, writer-in-residence at the United Arts Council of Raleigh and Wake County, wrote: "I think that the educational system definitely needs to reflect the diversity of the population in the United States. This is especially true for history and literature courses. Moreover, I believe that a mandatory course in cultural diversity would be especially helpful in that we all need to know about one another, including the positive contributions that the various ethnic groups have made in the United States. And, in addition, faculty members need to be sensitive to this concern."

Robert Shapard, professor at the University of Hawaii-Manoa, wrote: "Maybe such an inquiry (study) in this time of change can point toward some real improvements that could be made in the university system. ... Professors may be happy or unhappy (rightly or wrongly) but as long as changes go toward making the education of university students better, more power to you."

CONCLUSIONS

The following general conclusions can be drawn, based on results of the educator surveys:

1. Respondents tend to disagree that the business and education worlds operate on similar principles.
2. They overwhelmingly believe the current educational system needs to be improved.
3. They overwhelmingly believe that merit is an important component in the business and education worlds.
4. Unlike their business counterparts, respondents strongly support the idea of tenure, associating it more with academic freedom issues than lifetime employment.

5. Like their business counterparts, educators tend to reject the idea that business has its own tenure system with regard to unemployment benefits and severance pay. The question tested commonalities between the two systems, and both groups rejected this comparison for the most part. However, the large 30% neutral response by educators indicates a significant number of them may have felt unqualified to evaluate the business world, based on their work experience. Or perhaps some did not understand the statement or see any usefulness in their responding to it.

6. Educators overwhelming disagree that good and bad senior professors should be funded equally, according to rank. This underscores their commitment to the idea of merit. It also indicates that respondents reject the idea of seniority, or years in rank, as a foundation upon which to base salary. Unfortunately, however, seniority—as illustrated in Chapter 4—is a chief factor to determine paychecks in academe, according to a system that features near across-the-board annual raises off the base salary.

7. Respondents tend to disagree with the idea of lower-rank professors participating in the salary and promotion decisions of senior professors. At many institutions, including my own, lower-rank professors (including assistant professors) serve on personnel and annual review committees and evaluate senior professors for merit raises. Fewer institutions allow assistant professors to vote in promotion decisions. Respondents may believe that lower-rank professors are inclined to give senior professors high marks in annual reviews because their own tenure or promotion may be at stake. Or because tenure and promotion may be at stake, respondents may believe that administrators and other senior professors should be doing the evaluation at this level.

8. However, the respondents agree that lower-rank professors should evaluate department heads, who usually also are senior professors with great power to influence decisions about tenure and promotion. Respondents may be expressing the need to hold department heads accountable because their decisions affect everyone in the unit. Or respondents may assume that such reviews would be confidential, a protection that is difficult to provide in annual review committees that usually contain a mix of assistant, associate, and senior professors.

9. Respondents feel administrators should bolster morale when forced to make cutbacks.

10. Here is the profile of the typical educator who responded to the survey:

He or she thinks the business and education worlds operate on different principles. And yet the professor believes strongly that the current educational system needs to be improved. He or she believes that good work is rewarded in business and also should be rewarded in academe. According to this professor, tenure protects academic freedom and should be maintained. He or she really doesn't think that business has its own brand of tenure via unemployment benefits or severance pay. In fact, the professor may not see any need to make such a connection. In any case, he or she objects strongly to a merit system that funds good and bad professors equally, much like a union would, across the board and according to rank. The professor may feel some ambivalence with the evaluation system as it exists in academe, though. On the one hand, he or she believes that lower-rank professors should have little say in salary and promotion decisions that affect senior faculty. On the other hand, he or she thinks that lower-rank professors should evaluate their department heads. Morale is fair to low at his or her university, especially during cutbacks, and the professor holds the administration accountable.

Nine

THE GOVERNOR'S AIDE RESPONSE

[P]roblems are generally caused by systems, not people. ... This would indicate that
tenure is not the problem so many think it is in education. ..."

SCOTT FARRIS, Wyoming

RESPONDENTS

Fifty aides, or one from each state, were sent surveys and 22, or
44%, returned them. The respondents did not contribute many
comments, however. Of the seven who returned their surveys with
comments, six contained minor observations less than a paragraph in
length. Only one provided significant opinions, and of the 22
respondents who returned surveys, only three gave permission to use
their names and/or identify their states.

FINDINGS

Here is the survey that governor's education aides received with
tabulated percentages under each of the five responses of the Likert
scale: Circle the appropriate number under each question below:
1=Strongly Agree 2=Agree 3=Neutral 4=Disagree 5=Strongly Disagree
1. The business and education worlds operate on similar principles.

Strongly Agree	Agree	Neutral	Disagree	Strongly Disagree
0.0%	23.8%	0.0%	61.9%	14.3%

2. I think the current educational system needs to be improved.

Strongly Agree	Agree	Neutral	Disagree	Strongly Disagree
61.9%	33.3%	4.8%	0.0%	0.0%

3. I think merit (reward for good work) is important in business.

Strongly Agree	Agree	Neutral	Disagree	Strongly Disagree
47.6%	42.9%	9.5%	0.0%	0.0%

4. I think merit is important in education.

Strongly Agree	Agree	Neutral	Disagree	Strongly Disagree
38.1%	42.9%	9.5%	9.5%	0.0%

5. I think tenure (continual reappointment, with few stipulations) is an important aspect of higher education.

Strongly Agree	Agree	Neutral	Disagree	Strongly Disagree
0.0%	30.0%	20.0%	40.0%	10.0%

6. Benefits (unemployment/severance pay) create a kind of tenure for executives with seniority in the business world.

Strongly Agree	Agree	Neutral	Disagree	Strongly Disagree
0.0%	19.0%	28.6%	47.6%	4.8%

7. The best and worst senior professors should be funded equally, according to rank.

Strongly Agree	Agree	Neutral	Disagree	Strongly Disagree
0.0%	0.0%	0.0%	42.9%	57.1%

8. Professors of lower rank (assistant, associate) should evaluate senior professors to determine salary and promotion.

Strongly Agree	Agree	Neutral	Disagree	Strongly Disagree
0.0%	0.0%	50.0%	20.0%	30.0%

9. Professors of lower and upper rank should evaluate department heads.

Strongly Agree	Agree	Neutral	Disagree	Strongly Disagree
5.3%	31.6%	31.6%	26.3%	5.3%

10. Administrators should bolster morale when forced to make cutbacks.

Strongly Agree	Agree	Neutral	Disagree	Strongly Disagree
36.8%	47.4%	15.8%	0.0%	0.0%

In sum, over three-fourths of the governor's higher education aides disagree with the premise that the educational worlds and the business worlds operate on similar principles.

Nearly all respondents feel that higher education needs to be improved. There is 0.0% disagreement with the question and less than 5% have no opinion.

On the issue of merit, over 90% of the aides agree that the concept is important in business. Merit in education is also perceived favorably, with 81% of respondents in strong agreement or in agreement with that concept. Reward for good work is perceived to be slightly more important in business than education, however, with nearly 10% of aides disagreeing that merit should be an important component of academe.

The aides feel quite differently about tenure than they do about merit. Only 30% of the respondents agree that tenure is an important aspect of higher education. No aide strongly agrees with this statement. Half disagree or strongly disagree with the idea of tenure. Nearly one-fourth of the aides have no opinion on tenure.

Over half of the respondents disagree or strongly disagree that benefits (unemployment/severance pay) create a type of tenure in the business world. Almost 30% have no opinion on this issue. Less than 20% agree with the statement.

Respondents are in 100% disagreement with the statement that the best and worst professors should be funded equally. This response reinforces the merit issue, which they overwhelmingly believed was an important component in education.

The aides are less united in their response to the statement that lower rank professors should evaluate senior professors to determine the latter's salary and promotion. Half of the respondents disagree or strongly disagree with this practice. The other 50% are neutral about this form of evaluation.

Likewise, government respondents are nearly equally divided on the issue that professors of lower and upper rank should evaluate department heads. Thirty-seven percent agree with this statement while 31% disagree. The remaining 31% have a neutral response to this statement.

Finally, there is strong agreement (84%) with the idea that administrators should bolster morale when forced to make cutbacks. There is no disagreement with this statement and only 16% are neutral on this issue.

GROUP COMMENTS

Because comments were so scant, they cannot be broken down into categories as they were in the business and educator chapters. Neither can states that responded (or failed to respond) to the study be identified because the names of higher education aides are readily available from *The Chronicle of Higher Education Almanac* issue. Admittedly, this is a conservative (but ethical) view on privacy and disclosure.

In total, four aides had minor comments (less than a paragraph alongside a question or at the bottom of the survey). These did not grant permission to use their names. Two aides with similarly minor comments gave permission to use their names, and one aide gave permission and had significant comments and opinions.

Here are the complete comments of the anonymous aides:

— "It (merit in education) won't work although the concept has merit in my opinion."

— "It's part of any employer's job to bolster morale regardless of circumstance."

— "Many of the principles used in education and business are similar but a few are quite different, e.g., principles relating to complex organizations and profit vs. not for profit."

— "Not who evaluates whom—but on what basis. For too long, our evaluation methodology has not had any real value. Morale is an easily used word. It always comes up when faculty and adminstration are confronted by $ cutbacks, outdated programs and courses, lower enrollments, etc. It is the wolf cry and it has been heard too often."

These are the minor comments of aides who granted permission to use their names and identify their states:

— "While I do agree with the concept of merit pay, I have questions about the methods of awarding merit"—Jeanne Forrester, Mississippi.

— "I have strong views on all of the questions posed but I find insufficient info to respond. What would make a survey more meaningful would be a one-page summary of the purpose of the study, objectives, etc."—Charles E. Spath, New Mexico.

For the record, I did not enclose a one-paragraph summary of my article, "Academic Socialism," as I did in letters to the business and educator groups. Because I selected business and education leaders in a non-random, unscientific manner, I felt I could summarize my essay. However, because random selection was not a requirement for scientific validity with the governor's aide group, constituting an entire universe, I stressed objectivity in my accompanying letter.

Here is the text: "I'm a writer and professor at Ohio University researching the issues of merit and morale in higher education. The following letter and survey has been sent to 50 gubernatorial aides who handle higher-education questions. I not only am interested in your answering the survey but also in your comments—general or specific—

regarding merit and morale in higher education. Please take a minute to do this because, given the small number of respondents, I am hoping for a 100% response.

"Finally, feel free to write a personal letter if you feel strongly about any issue covered or not covered in the survey. You may also send me any data or publications that you have compiled and that may be useful in my research. Thank you for your time and consideration."

In the above letter, I mention twice that the study focuses on problems of merit and morale in higher education. In tandem with the accompanying survey, the objectives are clear: comparing the importance of merit in business and education and other issues such as tenure, across-the-board funding, and administrative responsibility to maintain morale. In addition, to ensure that the letter was objective, I asked two researchers at Ohio University to read it. Both said the letter was sufficient for a scientific response. Moreover, the letter clearly gives higher education aides the opportunity to send data or publications that may influence the research.

None did.

Only one aide, Scott Farris of Wyoming, shared his views in a substantial and enlightening way. Here is his comment reprinted in its entirety: "I have become a convert to the Total Quality Management principles espoused by Dr. Edward Deming (a Wyoming native, by the way) and believe a number of TQM practices can be applied to education as well as business. I do believe government, including education, should be run like a business—a good business. Unfortunately, that saying is often used to suggest government should operate like an unsuccessful business—one which does not plan, one which does not operate as a true system, one which does not focus on achievement, one which treats employees as something separate from the business.

"Central to Dr. Deming's beliefs are the notions that problems are generally caused by systems, not people, and that any organization must operate as a team, not a set of disparate departments or individuals. This would indicate that tenure is not the problem so many think it is in education. If there is a problem with a teacher, rather than simply suggest that person is lazy or stupid, Dr. Deming's philosophy would suggest that the teacher has not been adequately informed of his

141

or her mission and place within the organization, has not been given the flexibility to do the job using their best abilities or that they have not been properly selected or trained for the job. My own personal experience in business, government and education would sustain that view.

"Finally, on the idea of merit pay, I also subscribe to Dr. Deming's view that individual merit pay can be a poison in any organization. Individual merit pay provides an incentive for competent teachers—or any employee—to operate independently and to achieve at the expense of his or her peers. There would be no incentive for a good teacher to spend time to assist a poor teacher and make that teacher better. Merit pay should be on a school-wide basis at least to foster a spirit of teamwork, cooperation and mentoring that will ensure every teacher becomes better and that every student benefits. My own experience indicates that most employees only want to be treated fairly and equally. Less dissention is caused by occasionally giving an undeserving employee a pay raise that everyone receives than by singling out individuals for benefits when others believe they may be equally deserving or when they may question the criteria for this merit increase."

Farris, in answering my survey so completely, is practicing TQM by sharing his information.

CONCLUSIONS

These conclusions can be drawn from the survey sent to governor's higher education aides:
1. Aides clearly view the education and business sectors as operating on different principles.
2. Aides believe higher education needs to be improved.
3. Aides believe in the concept of merit, or reward for good work, as important in both business and higher education.
4. Aides do not believe tenure is important in academe. However, there is some indication that they might be receptive to arguments to maintain tenure.
5. Respondents do not equate unemployment benefits and severance pay

in business with the concept of tenure in academe.

6. Aides disagree that good and bad professors should be funded equally across the board. This response underscores their commitment to the concept of merit.

7. The large neutral responses to questions about evaluation methods in academe indicate that aides do not have strong feelings about the evaluation process to reward good work. Although aides identify with the concepts of merit and merit pay, they seem unsure how to institute them in higher education. Neither is there strong agreement on who should be evaluating whom—or what, for that matter. Perhaps they view this as something educators should work out for themselves.

8. Aides believe faculty administrators should bolster morale and be held accountable for maintaining it, especially during hard economic times.

9. Overall, aides seem reluctant to commit themselves, their governors, or their states when it comes to disseminating ideas about higher education. Three observations support this assessment: scant comments on surveys, general unwillingness to be identified, and total unwillingness to share useful information (task force reports, published data, etc.). The last item was particularly troublesome in that governor's education aides take stances generally closer to that of business people than of educators. In a word, sharing useful information (ideas on gain-sharing, for example) is a valid business practice. The aides' general non-commitment is also troublesome in as much as taxpayers fund reports and data about higher education. In sum, the no-comment agenda of the government sector may overshadow the commitment to contribute to or initiate a dialogue about academe.

10. The non-commitment of higher education aides in their comments, general unwillingness to be identified, and total unwillingness to share information, in some sense supports the need as expressed in Chapter Six, "Hybrid Studies," to search for new research models that elicit comments and opinions. Of the three surveys, only the governor's aide one was scientific and encompassed an entire universe, making the tabulated statistics highly reliable. At the same time, however, this perhaps is the least interesting and useful of the three studies because it generally is devoid of attitudes that spark debate and opinions that influence outcomes.

Ten

COLLECTIVE VIEWS AND
CONCLUSIONS

[A]bolition of tenure would radically change the character and qualifications of college and university faculties. Young people now typically spend five to six years earning a doctorate. ... Why would they do so if their training could be rendered useless by some administrator. ..."

JOHN C. MOORE, professor of History, Hofstra University

OVERALL RESPONSE

In sum, 49 business leaders, 83 educators, and 22 governor's higher education aides responded to the survey. They provided a total of 73 comments, with the most (37) coming from the educator group and the least (7) coming from the governor's aide group. The most popular topic discussed by respondents on the back of their surveys concerned methods of rewarding merit (31), followed by issues involving morale (19), the business-education relationship (18), and tenure (14). Of those making comments, a total 43 allowed the use of their names, with the most (23) coming from the educator sector and the least (3) from the government sector.

OVERALL FINDINGS

Here is the collapsed survey, combining statements from surveys sent to the three select groups—with variations in Questions 7-10 in brackets—showing the valid percentage response to each statement according the Likert scale:

Circle the appropriate number under each question below: 1=Strongly Agree 2=Agree 3=Neutral 4=Disagree 5=Strongly Disagree
1. The business and education worlds operate on similar principles.

Strongly Agree	Agree	Neutral	Disagree	Strongly Disagree
2.7%	20.0%	12.0%	44.0%	21.3%

2. I think the current educational system needs to be improved.

Strongly Agree	Agree	Neutral	Disagree	Strongly Disagree
50.7%	41.4%	3.9%	2.6%	1.3%

3. I think merit (reward for good work) is important in business.

Strongly Agree	Agree	Neutral	Disagree	Strongly Disagree
59.9%	32.9%	2.6%	1.3%	3.3%

4. I think merit is important in education.

Strongly Agree	Agree	Neutral	Disagree	Strongly Disagree
55.3%	34.2%	3.3%	3.9%	3.3%

5. I think tenure (continual reappointment, with few stipulations) is an important aspect of higher education.

Strongly Agree	Agree	Neutral	Disagree	Strongly Disagree
29.8%	29.8%	9.3%	19.2%	11.9%

6. Benefits (unemployment/severance pay) create a kind of tenure for executives with seniority in the business world.

Strongly Agree	Agree	Neutral	Disagree	Strongly Disagree
7.4%	19.5%	22.1%	41.6%	9.4%

7. The best and worst senior [employees, professors] should be funded equally, according to rank.

Strongly Agree	Agree	Neutral	Disagree	Strongly Disagree
1.4%	3.4%	2.7%	33.3%	59.2%

8. [Employees, professors] of lower rank should evaluate [each other's, senior professors'] job performance to determine pay scale and promotion.

Strongly Agree	Agree	Neutral	Disagree	Strongly Disagree
4.0%	12.0%	17.3%	31.3%	35.3%

9. [Employees, professors] of lower [and upper=*government only*] rank should evaluate their [managers, department heads].

Strongly Agree	Agree	Neutral	Disagree	Strongly Disagree
16.8%	39.6%	18.1%	16.8%	8.7%

10. [Executives, administrators] should bolster morale when forced to make cutbacks.

Strongly Agree	Agree	Neutral	Disagree	Strongly Disagree
43.4%	38.5%	14.7%	0.0%	3.5%

In sum, respondents of the three surveys disagree or strongly disagree (65%) that the business and education worlds operate on similar principles. Only 20% agree with this idea with a scant 3% agreeing strongly and 12% remaining neutral on the issue.

An overwhelming 92% agree or strongly agree that the current educational system needs to be improved. About 4% were neutral on this question and 4% disagree or strongly disagree.

An overwhelming 93% believe that merit is important in business and 90% believe that it also is important in education. Only 5% believe that merit is not an important business component (3% are neutral) and only 7% believe that merit is not an important educational component (again about 3% are neutral).

When respondents of all groups are measured together, about 60% agree or strongly agree that tenure is important, reflecting the attitudes of academics more than that of business or government. About 9% are neutral on the issue with the rest disagreeing (19%) or strongly disagreeing (12%).

Most respondents (51%) disagree or strongly disagree that business has its own tenure system with regard to unemployment benefits and severance pay. About 27% agree or strongly agree with this notion and 22% are neutral.

Respondents from all three groups overwhelmingly disagree or strongly disagree (93%) with the idea of funding senior personnel (employees=*business*/professors=*education* and *government*) equally, according to rank. This confirms the idea of merit in the three sectors. A scant 1% strongly agrees, 3% agree, and 3% are neutral on the issue.

Findings in Statement 8 reflect a general, overview of the role of authority and rank in three select groups. The business sector was asked to respond to the matter of lower-rank employees having a say about each other's job performance to determine salary and promotion, as many like-rank professors do in annual review and personnel committees; the education and government respondents were asked to respond to lower-rank professors evaluating senior professors for pay scale and promotion. The commonality in the issue for all groups was the fact that money and power would be partly determined in a business or academic unit by junior personnel. Respondents disagree or strongly disagree (67%) with such a notion with 17% neutral and a combined

16% agreeing or strongly agreeing.

Statement 9 varied slightly in each survey to test specific attitudes (teamwork=*business*/morale=*education*/accountability= *government*). Like Statement 8, this one also gauges the role of authority and rank in personnel matters, but without the pay scale and promotion factors. When such factors are removed, the negative response (67%) in Statement 8 nearly reverses itself in Statement 9, with 56% agreeing or strongly agreeing that junior personnel should have a say in the evaluation of their supervisors. About 18% are neutral on this issue, with a combined 26% disagreeing or strongly disagreeing to the practice.

A significant 82% of respondents believe that executives in business and their administrative counterparts in education have a responsibility to bolster morale when forced to make cutbacks. No respondent disagrees with the practice, although 4% strongly disagree and 15% are neutral.

Finally, while these findings provide an overall view of attitudes by all respondents who participated in the study, they do not indicate how each group influenced the combined-group tabulated percentages. To determine that, see Tables 1-10 in the Appendix which provide a clearer perspective, along with other information used to interpret conclusions below. In essence, the tables (or crosstabulations) were studied to isolate any significant differences in attitude between and/or among groups. A statistical test called the One Way Analysis of Variance was applied to each statement. When a significant difference was found, as happened twice with the above group responses, another statistical tool—the Post Hoc test—was applied to ascertain where, precisely, those differences lay. (Again, this is explained in the Appendix.)

The tests found that the educator group viewed the issue of tenure as expressed in Statement 5 favorably, differing significantly from the business and governor's aide groups, both of which tended to disagree that tenure was important in academe. The tests also found that the educator group tended to favor lower-rank professors evaluating their departments heads while the business group, usually quite decisive, remained uncommonly neutral about lower-rank employees evaluating their managers.

OVERALL CONCLUSIONS

Based on the overall responses by the three select groups, analyzed collectively and individually, general conclusions can be drawn that reflect the perceptions of the respondents:

1. All three select groups, in varying degrees, share these commonalities:

—Respondents disagree that the business and education worlds operate on similar principles.

—They agree that the current educational system needs to be improved.

—They believe that merit is important in business.

—They believe that merit is important in education.

—They disagree that tenure in academe correlates with unemployment benefits/severance pay in business.

—They disagree that good and bad senior professors or employees should be funded equally, according to rank.

—They believe that executives and administrators should be accountable for morale when forced to make cutbacks.

2. The select groups, in varying degrees, share these differences:

—Educators believe that tenure is an important academic concept, but business leaders and governor's aides do not.

—Business and education respondents disagree that junior personnel should be involved in decisions about pay scale and promotion of superiors. Half of the governor's aide sample also disagrees with this practice, but half also remain neutral, a remarkably high degree of non-commitment.

—When money and promotion factors are removed, educators believe that junior personnel should evaluate their department heads. Business respondents are surprisingly neutral on the issue. Governor's aides lean toward neutrality as well. This finding suggests that authority and rank play a greater role in the business and government sectors than in academe or may indicate, as this study theorizes, that administrators need to be held accountable, even by junior personnel.

3. These hypotheses, expressed in Chapter Six, were upheld by respondents included in this study:

—Respondents from the three groups tended to disagree that the business and academic worlds operate on similar principles.

—Respondents from the three groups tended to agree that higher education needs to be improved.

—Respondents from the three groups tended to agree that merit is important in business.

—Respondents from the three groups tended to agree that merit is important in education.

—Business and government respondents tended to disagree that tenure is an important academic concept.

—Educators tended to agree that tenure is an important academic concept.

—Business respondents who commented on the back of surveys would share their methods of rewarding merit. (This was by far the most popular topic with 18 of 29 respondents sharing one or more methods.)

—Educators who commented on the back of surveys would share their comments about morale in academe. (This was the most popular topic with 15 of 37 respondents sharing anecdotes or examples about unfairness contributing to low morale in academe.)

This hypothesis was partially upheld:

—Educators would differ significantly from business and government respondents in perceiving how the evaluation process rewards merit. (In fact, the only significant statistical difference was between the education and business sectors and involved only one aspect of the evaluation process; in sum, educators believed lower-rank professors should evaluate department heads whereas business leaders were divided and ultimately neutral about lower-rank employees evaluating their managers.)

This hypothesis was not upheld:

—Educators would tend to agree that executive seniority creates a kind of tenure in the business world. (Select educators tended to disagree with the comparison or see no need to make it, with a large 30% neutral response. Originally I felt that educators would strongly support tenure and thus would be eager to show business leaders that they, too, have job security built into their system. What I failed to predict, however— and this is a real discovery—is that professors did not tend to see tenure as job security but genuinely believed it to be a protector of academic freedom. More on this later.)

OBSERVATIONS AND RECOMMENDATIONS

The purpose of this study began as an attempt to enlarge the parameters of the education-reform debate set in 1987 by E.D. Hirsch and his book *Cultural Literary* and Allan Bloom and his book *The Closing of the American Mind.* I felt that these books had overinfluenced the debate because they failed to link the role of administrators to growing problems of merit and morale in academe. I believed that administrators were largely held non-accountable while the debate about higher education focused, in large part, on pop culture and the slackness of students and their professors. I published an essay about this titled "Academic Socialism," discussing administrators who pretended that everyone was "equal" when, obviously, everyone was not. I argued that merit, or reward for good work, was important to keep up morale.

Business and government leaders believe strongly in the idea of "merit." Whatever that word means, it does suggest that all professors are *not* equal and that good work should be rewarded in some or all of the ways possible right now within higher education. Good professors should earn higher salaries than mediocre counterparts. But money is not the sole incentive to motivate professors. Administrators can establish clearer roles, identities and goals for each faculty member so that everyone feels a sense of contribution to some overall vision or mission. Administrators not only should help formulate objective criteria to reward merit in tenure and promotion documents, but also should *oversee* the evaluation process so that annual review committees follow the P&T document.

The reward system for administrators also needs to be revised. Many do not receive incentives for managing their units but for procuring outside funding. The overemphasis on funding has turned many department heads, chairs, directors, and deans into office managers. They schedule meetings and classes, make committee assignments, answer memos and inquiries, consult with industry, and bring nearly every issue to the faculty for a vote. Of course I know that funding may be an important goal of any institution, especially private ones; but I know as well that all institutions have alumni associations and foundations already responsible for donations and solicitations. If outside funding is a priority, administrators—and faculty, for that matter—should be responsible for identifying potential contributors; perhaps administrators and professors should receive good marks for service when they do and be rewarded according to a specific P&T document. Above all, however, both should be held accountable for their *primary* roles. Professors are being held accountable by business and government who maintain that teachers should *teach*. What about administrators? Shouldn't they *administrate*?

At the least, administrators should motivate or supervise non-productive professors, squelch feuds, deal swiftly with problems, and apply knowledge to knowledge by hiring and placing individual faculty members into a mosaic that symbolizes a mission or vision. In turn, specific goals should be aligned with the next level of administration—directorships, deans, provosts, presidents—providing a support system for individual administrators and an identity for entire institutions.

Effective administration is much like good writing. It is dangerous to extend a metaphor, I realize, but the device also can help simplify a complex mosaic:

—Each professor is a word that contributes to a statement.
—Each statement is a department that contributes to a paragraph.
—Each paragraph is a school that contributes to a college.
—Each college is a chapter that contributes to a university.
—Each university is novel. Each novel contributes to the canon.

Right now at many campuses each professor is a statement unto himself or herself. Business and government leaders, not to mention journalists, have focused on that. But they have not focused on the *source* of the problem—ineffective leadership—and until they do, the problems we already have identified will worsen and morale will sink along with educational standards.

In a word, administrators should accept the responsibility or the consequences. When they resign their posts and return full-time to the professoriate, they should forfeit administrative salaries. Based on their performance, new contracts should be drawn between the ex-administrators and their direct superiors (deans, provosts, presidents, regents). Moreover, the savings should not be applied to the general fund but to the academic unit in question and used to reward or retain productive professors or help underpaid female and/or minority ones attain parity.

Moreover, a foundation for administrative reform should begin at the undergraduate level. To help determine merit and detect problems, students should provide exit interviews. Administrative support staff at each institution has personnel capable of designing inexpensive and effective exit interviews. They not only should be given to seniors upon graduation, but also to students who drop out of school. Comments and data about academic programs in general, and professors in particular, should be sent to the appropriate administrator and be used in part to assess unit goals and individual merit.

The so-called "demerit system" of academe should be abolished. Any extra work taken on by any professor, tenured or not, should be rewarded and supported at all levels. This includes committee work, which Fred Chappell in Chapter Eight calls "a sucker's game." When extra work fails because of forces over which the professor has little or no control, the professor still should be rewarded and supported. Academic socialists are all too eager to take credit when projects or assignments succeed. When they fail because of professorial incompetence, then the administrator who assigned and oversaw the professor also should share partial blame.

Administrators also should support and maintain a balance of career teachers, researchers, and teacher-researchers. Arguments about which is better for academe have been exaggerated by the media and mythologized by the legislatures. In actuality, career teachers develop the minds of students and steer them through the labyrinth of academe; career researchers educate or train students so that they can get fellowships or jobs, and teacher-researchers do both.

However, when academic units have too many career-teachers or career-researchers, the imbalance usually involves mismanagement at the administrative levels.

Administrators in general have much to learn from business when it comes to problem-solving and motivation. They also can adapt tenets from such popular philosophies as Total Quality Management or from more value-based (rather than results-oriented) practices by small and midsize businesses. In Chapter Five, I attempted to show how some of these can be adapted to fit academe. But my intent was merely to show that they can be adapted without undermining traditional educational values. Certainly, when it comes to educational reform, I do not have the answers—no one person should—but I can make pertinent observations and modest recommendations upon which others with more expertise may act.

That is why this book has two sections. I state my case in the first five chapters and then invite others to do the same. Even if you disagree with the theme of this book—that administrative non-accountability is ruining academe—I have tried to provide you with a wealth of information that can expand the parameters and redirect the focus of the education-reform debate.

Clearly, the qualitative/quantitative approach deserves more scrutiny. One of my goals was to expand the parameters of the education-reform debate, but another equally important one was to expand the parameters of what we call "research" in the social sciences. As an essayist and journalist, I devised an interdisciplinary model in my methodology for "Hybrid Studies." This, too, can be improved upon by others with more expertise.

In essence, I wanted to test my qualitative assumptions with opinion leaders who would support or rebut my arguments with as much or more expertise or eloquence. In return, respondents affirmed many of my "truths." The anonymous CEO defense contractor believes, as I do, that government is going to revamp higher education by decree unless educators put effective reforms into place very soon. Indeed, other business respondents echoed many of my concerns about merit and morale in the work place and some, like David J. Samuels, the retired Ohio Bell executive, affirmed my belief that instilling fear and blame "is the quickest way to lower morale" and reduce productivity. The comments of Thomas McKeon, vice president at the Citicorp Center in Taiwan, affirmed my belief that more can be done to reward and retain good professors. "You will not attract and retain good people," he maintains, until salaries and other benefits are equal to those in business. Moreover, McKeon offered a useful tip that all administrators should build into the infrastructure of academe: Establish clear paths to career opportunities, even when forced to make cutbacks. As McKeon indicates, times of challenge also can be times of achievement.

Further, Robert McDowell at Story Line Press in Oregon and Lynette Wood at Wood Advertising in Chicago also affirm my earlier observations about the spiritual values of small business and the morale-building contributions of pioneering women in the workplace. "Attend to the inner life," says McDowell. "Keep up on the lives of employees." Wood believes, "Executives have a responsibility to be human when making cutbacks," carefully separating economic issues from work-performance ones.

The comments of many educators affirmed some qualitative truths. The anonymous writer-professor who teaches at an institution in the Southwest focused exclusively on the issue of administrative non-accountability. He says that administrators operate "without a system of checks and balances" and "with little regard for the traditional purposes of their institutions." Moreover, Bollingen Prize-winner Fred Chappell's $25,000 annual salary after 20 years as an educator at a major university is testament to how the academic socialist system can ignore its most productive and able teacher-researchers. Several educators, including Gary Fincke at Susquehanna, called attention to lack of alignment between administrative goals and faculty rewards. Alicia Ostriker noted alongside a survey statement that excellent professors field offers from other universities, which "correlates loosely with merit." Finally, the comments of Judith Kitchen and Elton Glaser underscore the assumption that mediocre faculty will find ingenious ways to suppress productive professors. "Those professors who are not publishing will not willingly let me into their ranks to become their direct rival for raises and honors," Kitchen writes. Glaser affirms that mediocre professors consider "merit" a code word for inequality and elitism, resenting "those professors who get the promotions and the raises and the reduced teaching loads."

Mean-spirited professors wreak havoc because academic socialists let them.

Finally, comments by educators not only affirmed what I had believed but also informed me where I had gone astray: namely, on the issue of tenure. I had assumed that educators would be eager to compare the security of tenure with unemployment benefits and severance pay in the business world. Indeed, one educator, skittish in his tenure review year at an Illinois institution, made a similar comparison with senior employees close to retirement in the business sector. But then he elaborated on tenure, as did several others, associating it only with "freedom of speech and freedom to teach." Leonard Trawick in particular focused on the latter. "I would not want my job to depend on having to tailor my teaching and writing to fit the dogmas of a doctrinaire department head," he states. Thus, because of their comments and general rejection of Statement 6 on the survey, linking the security of tenure with business benefits, I theorize that many educators truly believe that tenure only protects academic freedoms.

However, this led to a chilling discovery. Several educators, including Reg Saner at the University of Colorado, linked political correctness to the purpose of tenure. As you may recall, Saner made and then later qualified this statement: "PC tongue-lock completes the vanishing purpose of tenure." Another respondent, the writer-professor who spoke of administrative non-accountability, called political correctness a "bloody" tool of administrators. Judith Kitchen spoke at length about how political correctness can influence one's grading and teaching: "God forbid we should act as though some students are 'brighter' than others, that some might actually be 'better' as students, for whatever reasons a good student is a good student. The PC movement has seen to that."

When I began this study, I knew that tenure was under attack by many business leaders and lawmakers. Typical of a journalist, I associated tenure with free speech *and* job security; in sum, in this book, I could challenge administrators, name my own and other universities, along with my governor, and be reasonably sure that I also would not be putting my own career or my family's security on the line. When I finished the study, however, I saw that tenure was not only under attack by business and government, but also indirectly from within, by educators themselves. If tenure indeed does grant professors only the freedom to teach what they please and to express themselves as they please, then political correctness, which attempts to influence the content of courses and the manner of speech, stands in direct opposition to this notion. Worse, the profile of the politically correct educator or administrator usually is opposite from the profile of the patriotic business person or conservative lawmaker who would abolish tenure. Simply, political correctness gives the latter one more reason and route to eliminate tenure without focusing on administrative accountability.

If tenure is abolished, the character of the university will change, but not necessarily for the better. One of the best arguments to convey this idea was made by John C. Moore, a history professor at Hofstra University, who published a letter in *The New York Times* in response to commentary against tenure, titled "Amid Joblessness, the Joys of Tenure" (*The Week in Review,* 12 December 1993). Moore noted that abolishment of tenure would allow administrators to fire otherwise productive professors, deciding they were "deadwood" at age 40.

Moore continued: "Accountants or lawyers who are fired in their 40's or 50's have a decent chance of continuing their professions elsewhere. There are hundreds of thousands of jobs for those occupations. But in the entire New York metropolitan area, there may not be a dozen jobs for a specialist in 18th-century French literature or Aristotelian philosophy. To fire such a person would be like disbarring a lawyer or denying a physician the right to practice medicine."[1]

Moore predicted that academe without tenure would be filled with generalists who can easily make the transition between the business and education sectors without serious financial losses. I predict that senior professors would be among the first to be fired, as they are often are in business, to meet budget cuts during recessions. But the business sector has the discipline of the bottom line and cannot cut productive employees who might earn a profit. The person to be let go in academe is just as apt to be the most productive who ruins the curve for others in the unit and who also may be unpopular because of that.

The academic socialist likes those odds.

To be sure, not all administrators are academic socialists. Many will read this book and realize that they do not fit the stereotype and may adopt or adapt some of my recommendations or ones by respondents to improve their management style or units. Academic socialists will have quite a different response, fuming because others will recognize them. These are people who will put into practice *any* reform as long as it is directed at others. They will say "yes" to anything business or government proposes or enacts. Afterward they will continue to mismanage their units and receive annual incentives for doing so, resigning when morale problems become too difficult to correct and taking with them their inflated salaries. Then they will write memoirs about the abuses of faculty during their administrations and retire with good pensions and emeritus status.

If tenure is abolished, and these abuses remain in place, these same academic socialists or their heirs will be happy to deal with unions invited to represent demoralized professors. Then they may negotiate with *total* disregard to merit considerations, diverting any remaining funds to support staff to make their own jobs easier or less stressful.

One of the dangers of academic socialism is that it makes faculty unions attractive. As the overall survey shows, all three groups— educators, business leaders, and governor's aides—generally reject the idea of across-the-board treatment of good and bad senior professors, according to rank. The combined overall responses also indicate a strong belief in merit. Indeed, there is much commonality between and among the diverse groups in this study.

Disagreement, basically, concerns tenure.

Now factor in the abolishment of tenure and the academic freedoms associated with it. Factor in continued administrative mismanagement, political correctness, and low morale. Factor in as well the quick fix that so many governors and lawmakers especially like during election years and tough economic times. The picture becomes clearer. If the above scenarios occur and then are allowed fester, how else in a meritless system to be rewarded except to correlate salary with rank? How else to protect jobs in a system that suppresses free speech?

Unions do those things exceedingly well.

I do not recommend this. I fear it. I would much rather see universities adopt and adapt merit models from business. I would prefer that lawmakers, regents and trustees focus on management problems within the academic socialist system. Moreover, I would rather professors speak with a unified voice and make their own case to the business sector, legislature, and media.

But I don't see that happening, either. Most professors, too busy teaching or researching to become involved in the debate—relying too much on tenure for that privilege—will likely complain about education reforms only after they have been enacted. Then these same professors will maintain that no one consulted them before instituting new policies.

Morale will sink to record lows.

If you are a professor who wants to improve merit and morale at the work place, you need to:

1. Rededicate your life to learning and service.
2. Enhance teaching or research.
3. Set goals and priorities for personal and/or group achievement.
4. Acknowledge different agendas and interests by other faculty members.
5. Celebrate your rivals' successes.
6. Celebrate your own successes by sharing your methods, publishers, or discoveries with other faculty members.
7. Stop feuding with colleagues or hiding out at home.
8. Evaluate colleagues fairly in equity and merit reviews.
9. Change your tenure and promotion document to reflect fairness.
10. Serve the student and the common good.

If you are an administrator, you need to:

1. Motivate professors.
2. Narrow their responsibilities.
3. Restore and maintain their identities.
4. Celebrate their outside interests.
5. Promote equality at the starting salary level and beyond.
6. Seek advice and welcome diversity.
7. Evaluate and reward fairly.
8. Modify the behavior of trouble-makers or problem-professors.
9. Emphasize teamwork and collegiality.
10. Serve the student and the common good.

The time to place blame already has passed. The time to influence the outcome of the debate has not passed, but it is running out. As I have tried to show here, seemingly diverse sectors of society often share more commonalities than differences. We may believe the worst about each other—that CEOs are ruthless, that professors are lazy, that governors and their aides are petty or opportunistic—but all of us believe higher education needs to be improved.

That's a foundation upon which good relations can be based. We need to trust and work with each other, if not for ourselves, then for the sake of students.

NOTES

1 "How Tenure Safeguards Academic Freedom," by John C. Moore, *The New York Times,* 22 December 1993, p. A12.

APPENDIX

CROSSTABULATIONS

Tables below are based on each survey statement, illustrating the range of responses (1=strong agreement, 2=agreement, 3=neutral, 4=disagreement, 5=strong disagreement) in percents by the select business, education, and government groups. Crosstabulations not only indicate how each group differs from or resembles each other, but also documents degrees by which they do so. Each question has five "cells" that correlate to attitudes of the Likert Scale above. Each horizontal row of cells shows the range of responses and each vertical row, the range among groups. Each row and cell has a role in interpretation, even empty (0.0%) ones, indicating broad, narrow, or split opinions within each group and/or in comparison to other. For example, you'll note a broad range of responses in the business and educator groups, which each contain only 3 empty cells out of 50. You'll note 16 empty cells in the governor's aide crosstabluation, indicating more conformity within the group in response to survey questions and a narrower viewpoint in relation to those questions.

Finally, as stated in the methodology section of Chapter Six, a statistical test called the One Way Analysis of Variance (ANOVA) was run on each combined set of responses to determine whether a significant difference in attitude existed between or among groups. The ANOVA found such differences in Tables 5 and 9 below. Then a Post Hoc test was applied to determine where specific differences exist. Thus, Tables 5 and 9 will contain a note for the lay reader explaining significant differences. Complete statistical information is provided for the researcher in Tables 11 and 12.

Table 1
Statement: The business and education worlds operate on similar principals.

	1	2	3	4	5
Business	2.1	12.8	12.8	40.4	31.9
Education	3.7	23.2	14.6	41.5	17.1
Government	0.0	23.8	0.0	61.9	14.3

Table 2
Statement: I think the current education system needs to be improved.

	1	2	3	4	5
Business	57.1	32.7	2.0	4.1	4.1
Education	43.9	48.8	4.9	2.4	0.0
Government	61.9	33.3	4.8	0.0	0.0

Table 3
Statement: I think merit (reward for good work) is important in business.

	1	2	3	4	5
Business	69.4	20.4	0.0	2.0	8.2
Education	57.3	37.8	2.4	1.2	1.2
Government	47.6	42.9	9.5	0.0	0.0

Table 4
Statement: I think merit is important in education.

	1	2	3	4	5
Business	55.1	30.6	6.1	2.0	6.1
Education	59.8	34.1	0.0	3.7	2.4
Government	38.1	42.9	9.5	9.5	0.0

Table 5*
Statement: I think tenure (continual reappointment, with few stipulations), is an important aspect of higher education.

	1	2	3	4	5
Business	6.1	22.4	10.2	32.7	28.6
Education	51.2	34.1	6.1	6.1	2.4
Government	0.0	30.0	20.0	40.0	10.0

*Note: The educator group differs significantly in its view of tenure from both the business and government groups. See Table 11 for complete statistical information.

Table 6
Statement: Benefits (unemployment/severance pay) create a kind of tenure for executives with seniority in the business world.

	1	2	3	4	5
Business	4.1	24.5	6.1	57.1	8.2
Education	11.4	16.5	30.4	30.4	11.4
Government	0.0	19.0	28.6	47.6	4.8

Table 7
Statement: The best and worst senior (employees, professors) should be funded equally, according to rank.

	1	2	3	4	5
Business	2.1	6.3	4.2	27.1	60.4
Education	1.3	2.6	2.6	34.6	59.0
Government	0.0	0.0	0.0	42.9	57.1

Table 8
Statement: (Employees, professors) of lower rank should evaluate (each others', senior professors') job performance to determine pay scale and promotion.

	1	2	3	4	5
Business	0.0	16.7	6.3	35.4	41.7
Education	7.3	12.2	15.9	31.7	32.9
Government	0.0	0.0	50.0	20.0	30.0

Table 9*
Statement: (Employees, professors) of lower (and upper = *government only*) rank should evaluate their (managers, department heads).

	1	2	3	4	5
Business	2.1	39.6	25.0	22.9	10.4
Education	28.0	41.5	11.0	11.0	8.5
Government	5.3	31.6	31.6	26.3	5.3

*Note: The educator group differs significantly in its view of this evaluation procedure from the business group only. The table illustrates a general, overall view of the role of authority and rank among the representative groups. See Table 12 for complete statistical information.

Table 10
Statement: (Executives, administrators) should bolster morale when forced to make cutbacks.

	1	2	3	4	5
Business	40.9	38.6	11.4	0.0	9.1
Education	46.3	36.3	16.3	0.0	1.3
Government	36.8	47.4	15.8	0.0	0.0

Table 11
Oneway Analysis of Variance
Statement 5: I think tenure (continual reappointment, with few stipulations), is an important aspect of higher education.

Source	D.F.	Sum of Squares	Mean Squares	F Ratio	F Prob.
Between Groups	2	113.6053	56.8026	46.7188	.0000
Within Groups	148	179.9444	1.2158		
Total	150				

Group	Mean
Educator[a][b]	1.7439
Government[a]	3.3000
Business[b]	3.5510

Groups with the same superscripts are significantly different at .050 level.

Table 12
Oneway Analysis of Variance
Statement 9: (Employees, professors) of lower (and upper = *government only*) rank should evaluate their (managers, department heads).

Source	D.F.	Sum of Squares	Mean Squares	F Ratio	F Prob.
Between Groups	2	17.0974	8.5487	6.3574	.0023
Within Groups	146	196.3254	1.3447		
Total	148				

Group	Mean
Educator*	2.3049
Government	2.9474
Business*	3.0000

(*) Denotes group significantly different at .050 level.

INDEX

PERSONS CITED IN THE WORK